Going South

I0806646

Bob Becker

Going South

Stories and Thoughts from a Northerner's Career as a Southerner

Illustrated by L. Azeo Torre
and Jane S. Brooks

PELICAN PUBLISHING
NEW ORLEANS

ISBN 9781455628551

Printed in the United States of America

Published by Pelican Publishing
New Orleans, LA
www.pelicanpub.com

To Patricia Becker, wife, mother, grandmother, teacher, truth teller, comforter-in-chief and my loving partner on this odyssey.

Contents

Foreword

This is a book of stories, and like most stories, they are about people, places, and experiences from real life. Ernest Hemingway is said to have written, "In order to write about life, first you must live it." These are my stories from my life, and not one of them is AI generated!

I've lived all my adult life in the Deep South—in New Orleans, Louisiana—despite growing up in the frigid north: Buffalo, New York. Not only did I live in Buffalo for twenty-one years, but I also spent two years in the Midwest at the University of Iowa as well as a few months in Baltimore, Maryland, between years in graduate school. In fact, my wife, Pat, and I had never been below the Mason-Dixon line until I went south to interview for a job. During my career in New Orleans, I became the director of the city planning commission, a senior manager at the Audubon Zoo and Park, and the chief executive officer of City Park.

It should come as no surprise that there are both stark differences and some similarities between Buffalo and New Orleans. For a good part of the year, Buffalo has cold weather and snow—lots and lots of snow and snowstorms. For a good part of the year, New Orleans has oppressive heat and humidity and is subject to hurricanes, heat waves and persistent flooding. Buffalo tends to be blue collar, with an emphasis on manufacturing and waterborne commerce from when Buffalo originally emerged at the end of the Eric Canal in the early 1800s. New Orleans got its start as a center of agricultural trade focusing on the Mississippi River and eventually became a center of oil and gas exploration. Both cities were populated by a variety of ethnic groups, including Germans, Italians, African Americans, and the Irish. Buffalo also featured members of the Polish and Slavic communities, while New Orleans contained Creoles, Cajuns, Native Americans and enslaved Black Americans. Moving from a childhood in Buffalo south to New Orleans involved a tremendous change in cultures, and some of the stories in this book reflect those differences.

After much thought and reflection about these changes and the life experiences that happened to me moving south, I began to think of writing them down when I retired and finished a first book, *New Orleans City Park: From Tragedy to Triumph*. That book contained stories, but I realized that there were many more interesting tales that were not included in that publication.

My original goal was to provide these stories to my children and grandchildren so that they would have a fuller understanding of my journey. On reflection, I certainly wish I had taken more of an interest in my parents' and other relatives' lives and experiences, but that opportunity was lost, and I didn't want to make the same mistake with my own family. I'm sure many people have a similar regret. But as I began to write and remembered more and more interesting experiences, I thought maybe there would be an audience for these short stories of a Northerner's journey in the South and of my odd career as a city planner, zoo manager, and park director.

Some stories merit only a few paragraphs, while others require more space for a complete retelling. As I think back on my life adventures that lend themselves to storytelling, I believe many readers will recognize similar experiences in their own lives.

I have grouped the stories into a variety of categories, and I have told them as I remember them. Many of these narratives are funny, while others revolve around Hurricane Katrina or my involvement with sports and so on and so forth.

I believe in the value of my stories because they reflect the challenges, opportunities, and experiences everyone, in one way or another, encounters in their journey through life. As Steve Jobs once said, "Your time is limited, so don't waste it living someone else's life."

I started out as a Buffalonian and, over the course of more than fifty years, ended up a New Orleanian. I had no choice in starting out as a Northerner, but I'm a Southerner by choice, and the stories in this book reflect this transformation. Along the way, I hope to impart a few lessons from my journey.

I'm glad to say that my life has been well lived, which is a tribute to Pat, my family, my friends, hard work, and a large amount of good luck. I hope you enjoy the adventures that happened to me. I know I have enjoyed remembering them!

The Wide World of Sports

"I must be in the front row!" —Bob Uecker

Bob Uecker's famous quote from a beer commercial where he tries to sit in a lower section of the baseball stands and is removed because his ticket is way up at the top of the stadium and he optimistically remarks that they must be relocating him to the front row kind of reflects my history with sports. I always felt I should do better at whatever sport I was trying. I played softball in various leagues when I was younger and even pitched in American Legion ball as a teenager. My father taught me how to bowl, and I bowled in leagues through college. I tried golf periodically, taking my clubs on a bus to the nearest course. In college, I even sold sporting goods in a store like Target. I tried sledding but never could get the hang of ice skating and couldn't afford skiing. I played street hockey, as did everyone in my Buffalo neighborhood. As adults, my wife and I bowled in a mixed doubles league, and I continued to bang my way around golf courses. But while I enjoyed sports, I was never "in the front row." The following sport stories reflect that reality.

A Baseball Story

When I was a sophomore or maybe a junior in high school,

I was part of a pickup baseball team that played American Legion ball. Most of the American Legion teams were made up of either regular high school teams or groups of employees from area companies. Needless to say, they were generally of high caliber. Not our team, which was made up of friends and friends of friends. A few played on high school teams, but mostly it was just kids from the neighborhood.

We had played a few exhibition games before the regular season started and myself and Joe Piacente were selected to be the starting pitchers. I was not very good and Joe not that much better, but we were better than anyone else, so it fell to us to pitch. Our very first game of the season came against a high school powerhouse: our own high school's team, the Kensington Knights. They competed virtually every year for the district and city championships, the school's athletic director was their coach, and their roster included several lettermen and All-High honor winners. I was selected to pitch the game for our team.

Kensington was up in the top of the first inning. They had on their high school uniforms, while our team was dressed as though we were in a street pickup game. My catcher, Phil Federico, who I believe went on to become an engineer, came out to the mound to give me a pep talk. It went something like, "You can do it! We are behind you! Just put it over the plate, and the guys will make the play behind you." I was not sure I could put a pitch over the plate and pretty sure my guys would not make the play if the ball was hit in their general direction, but there was nothing to do but throw it up there and see what happened.

Truth be told, I really had no effective pitches. I couldn't throw the ball very fast and had a pitiful pitch that was somewhere between a curveball and a slider. My control was good depending on the outing, but I wasn't confident I could get anybody out. The first batter came to the plate. The other team was yelling to cream the ball, while my team kept up a steady stream of meaningless chatter such as "Put it in there, Becker" and "Batter, batter, batter."

Incredibly, the first batter hit my second pitch—the first one being what the late Bob Uecker described in Major League as "a bit outside"—to our second baseman, who threw out the runner at first. So far so good, I thought. The second hitter, after fouling off a couple of pitches, popped up to our third baseman in foul territory. Two outs!

The third hitter, though, was another story. I knew him to be one of the top hitters in my high school (probably why he was batting third), and when he came to the plate, he looked like the mighty Casey with a bat that seemed to me to be a piece of lumber. This guy looked like a hitter, and his team just knew he was going to destroy me. I thought so, too. My first pitch was my pitiful curveball that barely made it to the plate but nevertheless was effective; he swung and missed. The next two pitches were balls. I threw the fourth pitch as hard as I could, and it was a called strike. (You're probably wondering how I can recall the exact pitches I threw almost fifty years after that memorable first inning. Sometimes when you're extremely stressed, the memories stay with you—and I was really stressed.) On the next pitch, he hit a ball so hard I thought the proverbial cover would come off the ball and kill his third base coach, but it was foul. On the sixth pitch, I once again summoned all my strength and threw my fastball on the inside corner of the plate, and he took a vicious swing but missed the ball. Strikeout! Unbelievable! As I came off the mound, Phil said, "Way to go, Becks. Way to go. I think your fastball was so slow, he couldn't adjust to it. Keep it up."

Our team, of course, could do nothing in the first inning as their pitcher looked like Walter Johnson in his prime. (Walter "The Big Train" Johnson was a major league pitcher in the twentieth century who was said to throw a ball so hard that you couldn't hit it because you couldn't see it.) Three quick outs and I was back on the mound.

Clearly, the Knights had done some talking about my pitching and were making adjustments. I got the first batter out, but then they began zeroing in on my two pitches, and when the inning was over, they had scored three runs. Still, I felt pretty good that I had gone a couple of innings and only given up three runs. I asked Joe if he wanted to come in and relieve me, but he said no thanks and that I was doing a fine job.

Top of the third. The wheels came off the bus. One time through the batting order was all Kensington needed to adjust to my pitches. No matter what I threw up there, they hit it. The inning seemed to go on forever. When it finally ended, they had scored eight runs and now led 11 to 0. When our team came up, again, we could not score. I came to bat and, frankly, was afraid of being beaned with the baseball; I managed only a weak grounder to second base.

We decided Joe would pitch in the top of the fourth. Before we could take the field, their coach, who was our physical education instructor in school, and the umpire came over to our bench. Our coach said that although there was no mercy rule in American Legion ball, he was prepared to call the game before anyone (read: us) got hurt or humiliated. But being proud ballplayers, we said we would soldier on—which we did, until Joe gave up eleven runs in the fourth. At 22 to 0, the umpire said we were done, and I said goodbye to my baseball pitching career—feeling pretty good that it took three innings to get eleven runs off me while my successor gave up eleven in one inning.

The Imposter

Did you ever consciously pretend to be somebody you weren't? I don't mean getting dressed up at Mardi Gras or playing cowboys and Indians when you were young—I mean in a professional or work situation. And I don't mean to limit the ruse to just masquerading as a different person—I also include pretending to have skills or abilities you didn't possess.

During my last couple of years in high school and throughout most of my undergraduate career at the University of Buffalo (now called the State University of New York at Buffalo), I had a part-time job at a company that resembled today's Target.

Twin Fair was a large big-box retailer that contained a grocery, a pharmacy, and a clothing department as well as jewelry and hardware sections. It had a toy department and a small cafeteria where you could get a sandwich or a whole dinner. It also had a sporting goods department.

When I first started at Twin Fair, I did the usual tasks, like bagging groceries, collecting the carts in the parking lot, unloading merchandise trucks, sweeping the floors, and so on. Eventually I was promoted to work in a specific department putting out merchandise, placing price tags on the merchandise (can you believe we actually put stickers on every piece of inventory we put on the floor?), taking inventory, and finally being on the floor as a salesperson. I started in the toy department but graduated to sporting goods.

I love sports, so naturally I was thrilled to be assigned to sporting goods, where I could help customers discern the difference between a baseball catcher's glove and a first baseman's or help a prospective hockey player pick out a defenseman's stick as opposed to the one a goalie used. I sold footballs, baseballs, volleyballs, football shoes, baseball cleats, dart sets, croquet mallets, bats, bowling balls, and even, in those days, a few soccer balls. The biggest sellers, however, were firearms, ammunition, and fishing equipment.

Now, I was excellent at selling items I was familiar with because I either played the sport whose equipment I was hawking or I was familiar with the sport from watching it on television. Not so much firearms and fishing gear. My father never took me hunting or fishing because he never went hunting or fishing. I never went camping except for a short stint in the Boy Scouts—I guess because we didn't have a car until I got to high school or maybe just because my dad didn't do those activities with his dad. At any rate, I knew virtually nothing about hunting or fishing, which is a big problem for a salesman selling those items.

One day, the store manager convened a meeting with everyone in the sporting goods department, including the full-time manager and the part-time sales staff. He told us that the regional sporting goods manager was unhappy with the sales in our store and had told the store manager he must develop new initiatives to boost sales. You know what rolls downhill, right? So that message was delivered to the store manager, who delivered it to the sporting goods department manager, who delivered it to his part-time sales staff. We were told to be more aggressive and to push sales, particularly of firearms and fishing gear, which had high profit margins. The sporting goods manager said he assumed we were all familiar with the fishing and firearms products and to make sure the customers knew how knowledgeable we were as we pushed sales. The implied threat was that if sales did not increase, he would find people who could make that happen.

As you already know, I didn't know the difference between a shotgun and a BB gun or between a fly-fishing rod and a regular fishing reel. While I attempted to look through some outdoor catalogs and magazines, I quickly realized I would never be able to make up my knowledge deficit without using any of the products I was selling—and that was not going to happen. So I did what everybody (or almost everybody) did when they didn't know something: I faked it.

When a fisherman came in and inquired about what type of fishing lure would attract bass, I said, "Why, I would try the Zoom tail lure or a spinner bait"—or any description on the lure package I could find. "What type of reel would you recommend for going fly-fishing?" "I would try the Zebco or Wilson reels—a lot of people have had success with those." "I'm going deer hunting and need a good Remington rifle. What would you suggest?" "Well, I would recommend the .30-06 as a fine piece of hunting equipment." As if I knew. "If I'm going squirrel hunting, what would you suggest?" I started off recommending a shotgun until more knowledgeable hunters said that was absurd. "Quite right, let's try a .22 or a BB gun." I once recommended a .300 magnum rifle for hunting pheasant—until I was told it was a big game weapon. Same with handguns. "I need a gun for protection." "Well then, you need a Smith & Wesson or a Glock high-capacity hard-hitting weapon." What about ammunition? I once recommended 12-gauge ammo for a 16-gauge shotgun.

One evening, a gentleman came into the store with his young son, maybe twelve years old. He came to the counter where my partner and I were waiting on customers and told us he was a deer hunter and wanted to outfit his son for a hunting trip. My partner thought this was a great opportunity to boost sales, so we recommended winter hunting gear, including a hat, leggings, winter boots—the whole shebang. Then the father asked what kind of weapon we would recommend for his son. Without missing a beat, my partner reached under the counter and pulled out a bowie knife. I grabbed the knife, and with my back to the father and son, said to him, "You can't give a bowie knife to a twelve-year-old to hunt deer with"—even I knew that!

I did my best to learn from my customers when they questioned my recommendations and offered advice. But basically, I was masquerading as a hunting and fishing professional—an impostor. I often wondered if anyone actually caught any fish with my fishing gear recommendations or had a successful hunt with a weapon I suggested. Oddly enough, no one ever came back complaining about a recommendation they received, and sales apparently went up, because I never heard from the regional sporting goods manager again. I'm not proud of this aspect of my career, but as they say, you do what you have to do!

The Golf Tournament

Like many public golf courses, the course at Audubon Park in New Orleans was often the scene of tournaments and fundraising events for churches, schools, companies, and a wide variety of other types of organizations. In general, these events go off without a hitch—but not always.

One of my responsibilities at Audubon Park was to oversee golf course operations, including special events. One day, as I was sitting at my desk, I got a phone call from a park neighbor who was complaining about the actions of various golfers playing in a tournament. The Audubon course is small (par 62 today) and in very close proximity to houses abutting the park and the golf holes. It is easy to observe play on the course from a number of those houses, and one of the neighbors was upset at what she was seeing.

Very often, golf tournaments provide food and entertainment, and this tournament had both. At the completion of the eighteen holes, there was a band and a crawfish boil to reward golfers who played the entire tournament. In addition, each of the eighteen holes had a sponsor, and food and beverages were offered at most of the greens so that as the golfers went from hole to hole, they had ample opportunity to consume not only the food but also alcoholic beverages. After a while, the social aspects of golf began to take precedence over the actual play.

At one of the holes, closest to the houses, the tournament sponsor had come up with an enhancement to the normal food and beverage offerings. They hired young women to act as "greeters" to the golfers who were coming onto the green to putt. These girls, who wore halter tops and short shorts (think Hooters outfits), interacted with the golfers and socialized with them during their time on the green. Apparently, the girls also tried to help the golfers with their putting by sitting on the green and spreading their legs to surround the hole. As each golfer putted, the girls would adjust their sitting position so that the ball would hit their thighs and roll up to and into the hole. Everyone except the neighbor thought this was hysterical, and as time went on, the more "expressive" the girls became, making this hole a favorite among the players. You get the picture.

The neighbor was emphatic over the phone. "Do you know what these girls are doing on the golf course?" she roared. "It's pornographic! Audubon is a public course in the middle of a public park, and I can't believe you're allowing this type of behavior that is so visible to park visitors. You have to do something!"

Of course, I had no idea that this type of activity was going on, but I assured the neighbor that I had not given permission for this type of behavior and did not condone it. I told her I would go right out and investigate her complaint.

Grabbing a golf cart, I went out onto the course and to the hole in question. It was not difficult to find as the various performances on that green had attracted quite a crowd. I told the girls they had to limit their greetings to waving hello and offering food and drinks to the golfers. They promised to comply. I'm sure I was the most unpopular Audubon official with the hole sponsor that day—not to mention the golfers!

Bowling Pin Setter

When I was growing up in the 1950s and '60s, Buffalo, New York—along with Akron, Ohio, and Detroit, Michigan—was pretty much the epicenter of professional tenpin bowling. It was wildly popular in northern cities, and everyone knew the names of the great bowlers of the era. Names like Don Carter, Billy Welu, Carmen Salvino, and Ray Bluth dominated the Professional Bowlers Association, which was formed in 1958. The professional bowlers tour began to be shown sporadically on television in the early 1950s. Buffalo never had a professional baseball team, and it had no professional football team until it secured a franchise from the upstart American Football League in 1960, so bowling had an outsized following.

Most of my father's friends that I was aware of bowled in leagues, sometimes as many as three or four nights a week. My father bowled in at least two leagues and was considered an outstanding bowler, just below the professional ranks. He had a variety of trophies and owned several bowling balls, something highly unusual for that time. Once in a while, my mother and I would go down to one of the alleys (there were many bowling alleys back then) and watch him bowl. I became attached to the sport and bowled in at least one league regularly through college, as did most of my friends.

While Gottfried Schmidt is credited with inventing the first mechanical bowling pinsetter back at the beginning of the twentieth century, that device wasn't universally in use until the 1960s. Before the automatic pin-setting machines, bowling alleys as well as recreation centers and even churches used pin boys to set and reset the pins as they were knocked down. I became a pinsetter at St. Gerard Church when I was about twelve. A friend and I, always on the lookout to make some spending money, applied when the church (which had a total of four lanes in its recreation hall) advertised the position. My dad, the bowler, thought it was a great idea. I really had no idea what the work entailed, but jobs for twelve-year-olds were rare, and it sounded like fun.

What did the job entail? At that time, the pin boys sat in a somewhat protected area adjacent to the pins. When the bowling ball knocked over some pins, you jumped down into the pit, swept aside the knocked-over pins, reset the rack that held the pins, put the bowling ball back on the chute that sent the balls back to the bowler, and then jumped into your protected position to wait for another shot. Sounds easy, right?

The entire process was frightening: grown men throwing a sixteen-pound sphere of rubber as hard as they could, which made a horrific sound when it struck the pins—and the pins did not always stay in the alley. Often, the force of the ball striking the pins was so great that the pins would fly up into your protected area, hitting you in all sorts of places. Despite every effort to protect yourself, you were constantly being struck by errant pins. Sometimes after a night of beer drinking (beer being Buffalo's accepted bowling beverage), the bowler would get anxious, not see that you were still in the pit picking up the pins, and launch another ball down the lane. This was very dangerous when it happened, and it usually happened once a night. You had to be alert, or the consequences would be severe.

At the end of the evening, after forty or fifty games, you went home full of bruises. I lasted about a month before my mother insisted I quit. I didn't need much urging to call a halt to my pin-setting career. My health seemed more important than a few bucks!

The New Orleans Saints and the Buffalo Bills

The cities of Buffalo and New Orleans, despite being more than one thousand miles and light years apart in terms of climate and culture, have one thing in common: they are both sports towns. Their fans are devoted to their sports teams, and both have been long-suffering, hoping against hope to be world champions at something someday.

Buffalo got its first professional football team, the Buffalo Bills, in 1960 when it became a member of the American Football League, eventually winning its championship in 1964 and 1965. When the older National Football League merged with the upstart American Football League in 1970, Buffalo became part of the NFL. The Bills have played in an outdoor stadium since entering the league and currently play in Highmark Stadium in the suburb of Orchard Park, New York. As of this writing, the Bills are building a new stadium, which will also be in suburban Orchard Park and will also be an outdoor stadium, despite Buffalo's horrendous winter weather. Building a new outdoor stadium probably dooms the community to never hosting a Super Bowl. (I'm sure you've all seen pictures of Bills fans in their stadium after a typical Buffalo blizzard, shoveling snow off the seats so the scheduled football game can be held. A few years ago, a crucial home game had to be relocated to Detroit when the snow made conditions unplayable.)

In 1970, the city also acquired its professional hockey franchise, the Buffalo Sabres, as well as a professional basketball team, the Buffalo Braves. The Sabres still play in Buffalo, although they

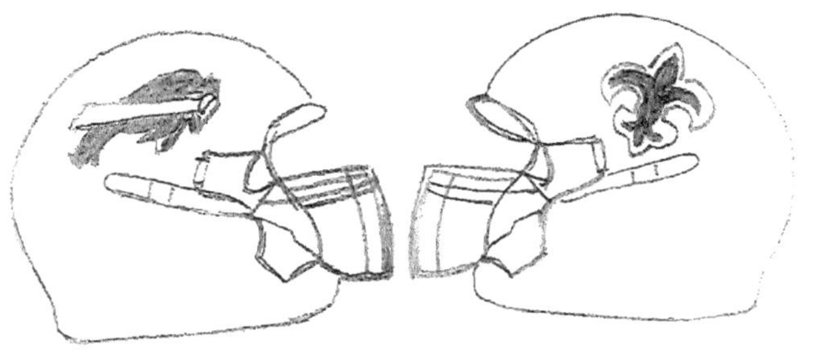

have never won hockey's ultimate prize, the Stanley Cup. The Braves basketball team played until 1978, when it left, ultimately becoming the Los Angeles Clippers.

Even though the Bills have never won a Super Bowl, the city loves its team, and their games are usually a sellout. The Bills have come close to a championship a number of times, most famously—or infamously—from 1990 to 1993, when they went to the Super Bowl for four straight years without winning the big game. The closest they came in that stretch was Super Bowl XXV with the New York Giants in January 1991. Buffalo had a chance to win the game in the final seconds, but Scott Norwood, the Buffalo kicker, missed a forty-seven-yard attempt with eight seconds left in the game, which went wide of the goalpost on the right side. The phrase "wide right," made famous by television announcer Al Michaels, has since been enshrined in Buffalo lore. (Ironically, over thirty years later, the phrase made another appearance in a Buffalo game when Buffalo kicker Tyler Bass missed a game-tying field goal in the AFC Divisional playoff game against the Kansas City Chiefs. How was the field goal missed? Wide right!) Unfortunately, Buffalo hasn't reached the big game since the early 1990s, disappointing an entire generation of Bills fans. (In spite of making first-team All-Pro in 1988 and leading the NFL in scoring, Norwood was waived after the 1991 season and never played football again.)

New Orleans's football team, the Saints, joined the National Football League as an expansion team in 1967 and played their first eight seasons in outdoor Tulane Stadium before moving into the enclosed Louisiana Superdome in 1975. They have played in the Superdome for fifty years and undertaken massive renovations to keep the stadium up to NFL standards when it comes to both customer amenities and football requirements. The Superdome hosted the Super Bowl in 2025, the eleventh time this mega event has been held in New Orleans. Like Buffalo's, this team has had traumatic moments in its history, the most famous being the "no call" when officials missed an obvious pass interference penalty against the Los Angeles Rams in the January 2019 National Football Conference game that would have sent the Saints to the Super Bowl.

The New Orleans basketball team was a founding member of the American Basketball Association in 1967, but poor play and the lack of a suitable arena led the team to relocate to Memphis. After the NBA granted an expansion franchise to the city and the owner of the Charlotte Hornets transferred the entire franchise there, the team became known as the New Orleans Hornets in 2002. Despite being temporarily displaced to Oklahoma City by Hurricane Katrina, the team was eventually purchased in 2012 by Tom Benson, the owner of the Saints, and renamed the New Orleans Pelicans. The team has never won an NBA championship, but unlike Buffalo, New Orleans still has a team.

New Orleans has never had a professional hockey team and has therefore never won the Stanley Cup.

The histories of the professional sports teams in the two cities are remarkably similar, except when they aren't. The Bills play in an outdoor stadium in a suburban location and are doubling down on an outside venue for their new stadium. The Saints have played in an indoor stadium in a downtown location since 1975 and are doubling down on that stadium with multiple renovations. Both teams began playing football in the National Football League within a few years of each other.

Both cities have had professional basketball teams that have never won a championship. New Orleans still has its team, while Buffalo does not. Buffalo has a professional hockey team but not New Orleans.

The most obvious difference between the cities is that New Orleans has a football championship, which it won in 2010 by beating the Indianapolis Colts (and their quarterback, New Orleans native Peyton Manning), and Buffalo, despite going to four consecutive Super Bowls, does not. In over fifty years of play, New Orleans has won one professional sports championship, and Buffalo has won none. Despite such dismal records, both cities follow their teams with fanatical devotion. Pat and I have attended many Saints games but left Buffalo having never attended a Bills game.

Where Were You on September 25, 2006?

Hurricane Katrina struck the city of New Orleans on August 29, 2005, and it caused massive damage to the Louisiana Superdome, the venue where the city's professional football team, the New Orleans Saints, played its home games. The roof was partially ripped off the stadium, causing massive flooding inside even as the facility was being used by thousands of citizens as a shelter of last resort. It would be many days before those occupants could be relocated outside the flooded city. The Saints and the National Football League quickly realized that the Superdome needed extensive repairs and could not be used for the 2005 regular season, which was shortly to begin.

After making hasty arrangements, the Saints played their home games on the road, splitting them between their temporary headquarters in San Antonio and LSU's stadium in Baton Rouge. They even played their first home game at the New York Giants stadium. To no one's surprise, the season was a disaster: the team recorded its worst record since its 1-15 season in 1980. Matters were not helped much by the constant rumors that owner Tom Benson was trying to move the team permanently to San Antonio, a move squashed by the NFL.

As the entire city struggled to recover, the 2006 football season got off to an inspirational start when the team hired a new football coach, Sean Payton, and took a chance on injured quarterback Drew Brees. The Superdome was repaired after a heroic effort by the State of Louisiana and the Saints and was ready for the team to compete in September. Our children had bought Pat and me season tickets for 2006, which was a total surprise—but one we were grateful for since we, like everyone in the city, wanted to rally around the Saints and show the NFL that New Orleans could support its professional franchise despite the hurricane's devastation of the city.

The Saints opened the regular season on the road against the Cleveland Browns and came away with a 19–14 victory. For week two, the team traveled to Lambeau Field in Green Bay to play the Packers, who'd beaten them the season before, 52–3. Drew Brees—showing why the decision to invest in him despite his coming off major shoulder surgery was the best personnel move in the history of the franchise—led the team to a 34–27 victory. We were on a roll, and the city was excited.

On September 25, the team returned from two road victories to the Louisiana Superdome, its first appearance there since December 2004. It was to be a Monday night game against division rivals the Atlanta Falcons before a sold-out crowd of seventy thousand raucous fans. Rock groups Green Day and U2 performed a pregame concert inside, while the Goo Goo Dolls held a concert outside the stadium earlier in the evening. Former President George H.W. Bush was part of the coin toss ceremony. The entire scene was pandemonium.

There was no way Pat and I were going to miss this game. Even though one-third of our house had flooded during Katrina and was uninhabitable and we were both working long hours and hoping we'd still be employed by year's end, we made our way downtown to the Superdome. Going into the game, much of the city was still in ruins, many houses were boarded up, and the future of health care, schools and employment was still in doubt. The fact that the Saints were able to return to the Superdome and play a football game seemed to take on a meaning that dwarfed the game itself. We saw several friends as we made our way to our new seats in the terrace section of the Dome around the twenty-yard line. Everyone was yelling and hollering, and the sound was deafening when the team took the field. The atmosphere was electric. It was Monday night football, for heaven's sake, and the game was broadcast by Cris Collinsworth and Miracle on Ice legend Al Michaels.

The national anthem was sung by New Orleans legends Irma Thomas and Allen Toussaint, and the Saints took the field with receiver Joe Horn leading the team. We were playing with a new coach, a new quarterback, and, for all intents and purposes, a new stadium.

It seemed like the crowd had just settled into their seats when the Saints defense blunted Atlanta's first possession, forcing them to punt the football. As the Atlanta kicker Michael Koenen received the ball from his center, the middle of the Atlanta offensive line seemed to open up, and special teams player Steve Gleason burst through the line and blocked the punt. Another special teams player, Curtis Deloatch, recovered the blocked punt and ran into the end zone for a touchdown. The crowd went wild, and the entire play seemed to symbolize the recovery not just of the football team but also of the city.

The Saints went on to win the game 23–3, win the NFC South Division title, and beat the Eagles in the divisional round before losing to the Bears in the Conference Championships. Pat and I will always remember the September game as giving us and the rest of the city hope that New Orleans had a future—and we were going to be a part of it.

Loss of Consortium

Large urban parks are sued constantly. It comes with the territory. When you have a specific area that receives hundreds of thousands or even millions of annual visits, you can be sure that not all those visits will go well. In parks, there are a plethora of reasons why your visit might not go as anticipated. You came for a special event or concert, and it's sold out. You can't find a place to park near the attraction you planned to visit. An unfilled pothole caused you to lose control of your bicycle, resulting in a crash and injury. Your picnic was ruined by raccoons that stole your food. You went to an amusement park, and your favorite ride was closed for maintenance. Someone let their dog off its leash (or never had it on a leash in the first place), and the dog threatened you or even bit you or your dog. You tripped and fell over a tree root or a crack in the sidewalk. As you were enjoying a relaxing time sitting on a bench or the grass, other visitors arrived, set up their boom box, and started belting out loud music. Sometimes it seems like there are a thousand reasons for a disappointing park visit.

When this happens, park officials try to put the best light on the visit by apologizing, handing out free tickets to a venue or event, or paying for repairs to a bicycle or vehicle damaged by park infrastructure gone bad. Sometimes, the police have to be called to settle disputes among park visitors that ruined the visit for both parties.

However, when all these solutions fail to satisfy, aggrieved visitors often resort to the court system. At any given moment, there can be multiple suits pending against the park—some of which have been pending for years. Such was the situation in City Park in 2001 when I became CEO.

Shortly after arriving at the park, I was contacted by the state attorney general's office concerning one such pending lawsuit against the park. (Because City Park is a state agency, the state often defended the park in what it termed "routine slip and fall cases.") This lawsuit, which stemmed from an incident that occurred in the late 1990s, had been winding its way through the legal system for years and was now nearing resolution. The state had a new assistant attorney general assigned to the case, and she wanted to understand the details before appearing in court for the next hearing.

The case involved one of the park's four eighteen-hole golf courses and an injury claimed by a non-golfing visitor who was passing by the course. (Now you know the reason this story is in the sports section!) For those familiar with City Park, the golf course in question was the old South Course, which was the first course opened in the park in 1902. Users of this course, which was closed in 2005, remember it as one where you could learn how to play the game because there were few sand traps and the holes were not particularly long, especially by today's standards. One of the holes ran parallel to an interior park road adjacent to the parks administration building. Because the hole was so close to the road and the road was used not only by vehicles but also by joggers, runners, and walkers, the park placed signs along the road warning users that there was active golf being played nearby. Of course, good golfers would never hit a golf ball into the road because they could place the shot onto the putting green, which was nearby. But not everyone who played the South Course was a good golfer. In fact, many players were poor golfers who could not control their shot and therefore couldn't guarantee that the golf ball wouldn't find its way to the road—hence the signs warning park patrons about the potential of having to dodge an errant golf ball bouncing toward them.

One weekday, a foursome of golfers came to the hole by the administration building, and one of them hit a shot that sliced to the right—missing the green entirely—bounced on the road, and struck a jogger who happened to be coming over a bridge. Of course, the ball could have hit the jogger in the arm or leg—but no, the ball struck him in the groin, causing him to double over and fall down.

While it did not appear to the golfers that the man was seriously hurt, a week before the one-year anniversary of the incident, the jogger filed suit against City Park for allowing a dangerous situation to exist that caused him grievous harm. However, he was not the only one who filed suit. His wife also filed a separate cause of action against the park alleging that because her husband was struck in the groin, she had suffered a loss of the benefits a spouse is entitled to from their partner, including companionship, affection, and, most importantly, sexual relations—in other words, a loss of consortium. The wife claimed that her husband had become reclusive and did not want to have sex with her, to the point that she intended to file for divorce.

The case dragged on for years, with the attorney general

asking for medical records and sworn statements from the litigants and an investigation into the couple's relationship prior to the incident. The park's principal defense was that it had put up signs warning park users that golf was being played close to the road and roadway users should beware. The couple eventually did divorce, although it was far from clear that the golf ball incident was the cause. Then the case went silent for several years, with neither the park nor the aggrieved couple taking any action to move the case forward. Allegedly, the husband moved out of state.

Our new assistant attorney general wanted to end this litigation, which was more of an irritant to her than anything else. Eventually, the court decided that the park had fulfilled its duty to warn park users of a potentially dangerous situation by posting warning signs and that park users were on notice to be vigilant when using any portion of the park and dismissed the case.

I immediately made sure the signs were still in place and had new signs put up anyplace I thought a park user might encounter an errant ball. The attorney general also recommended that any renovations to any of our courses should be done under the supervision of a licensed golf course architect, who could be sure any redesign would be done with the safety of nearby users in mind—which, of course, we did when we designed a new course following Hurricane Katrina.

Loss of consortium from a golf ball—who knew!

Lagniappe: Do you ever wonder who "they" is? You know—they. "They say you should drink more water" or "They say you should drive your car at high speeds every few months to keep the engine in good shape" or "They say to feed your dog raw meat" or "They said the avocados at the grocery store were old." Who the heck is "they"? In the age of artificial intelligence, how do you even know if "they" is the real "they" or whether it is a fake "they"? Or maybe "they" is everyone you want to agree with, whether you have the facts or not!

The Public Servant

"Do not let what you cannot do interfere with what you can do." —John Wooden, legendary basketball coach

The great majority of my career has been as a public servant, first as a city planner with the New Orleans Planning Commission and culminating with running a major urban park. Since the Audubon Nature Institute where I worked managing Audubon Park and Zoo is a nonprofit entity, you might lump that in as well and say my entire career has been spent serving the public in one form or another.

Being in the public eye and answerable in one way or another to the public is a great responsibility and often puts one in totally unexpected positions. The following are a few stories from my experiences as a public servant.

Pigs in the Canal

I was fortunate in that when I joined the New Orleans Planning Commission in June 1971, I was placed in the capital budget section, which was responsible for recommending projects that would go in the city's annual construction program. As a result, I got to travel across New Orleans visiting many of the city's public buildings, parks, neighborhoods, streets, and bridges as well as seeing capital projects from other independent agencies that impact the city. One of those agencies was the Sewerage and Water Board of New Orleans, which, as the name implies, is responsible for sewerage and water facilities. It is also responsible for major drainage facilities such as pump stations, main distribution lines, and large canals, which carry rainwater from city streets to pump stations that then pump the water out of the city. (New Orleans's topography is like that of a bowl, the bottom being below sea level, which means rain falling on the city must be pumped out of the bowl since it doesn't drain naturally.)

Through my work on the capital budget, I also learned a great deal about land use throughout the city and how the development of land interacts with the capital facilities supporting that development.

One day, after I had been with the commission for several years, my boss, planning director Harold Katner, called me into his office. He told me he'd had a call from the director of the Sewerage and Water Board (S&WB) asking for his help with an issue the board was having with the Vietnamese community in eastern New Orleans. During the 1960s and '70s, a large Vietnamese community had grown up in the suburban-like setting of eastern New Orleans, many of whom were refugees from the Vietnam War. They were a thriving and growing community with schools, churches, markets, and housing. The Catholic diocese ministered to the community and often helped the residents overcome language barriers. The Vietnamese were extremely resourceful in establishing local businesses and services for their community.

The S&WB's problem involved their drainage canals in the area. It seemed that many Vietnamese were used to farming on their property or in unoccupied lots and public spaces, just as they had always done in their homeland. They also kept a variety of farm animals, including chickens, cows, and pigs. The large drainage canals with their grass slopes were ideal for planting crops and allowing animals, particularly the pigs, to roam freely, feeding on the grass. The hot and humid southern climate made the canal banks ideal for such tenant farming activity.

However, when it rained, the canals rapidly filled up with water, as they held the water until the pump stations could kick in and drain it. During this time, the water was very deep and moved swiftly. It was dangerous, and if anyone fell into a canal, they would be at risk of drowning. The Vietnamese routinely tended to their crops and animals in the canals, and the S&WB was extremely worried that eventually, someone would be hurt or even killed when it rained, which in New Orleans happens pretty frequently. In addition, the farm animals, particularly the pigs, were damaging the canals as they rooted through the soil and destroyed the structural integrity of the banks and, therefore, the canals themselves. Officials from the S&WB had gone out to the community and tried to inform the residents about the dangers of farming in the canals, but apparently, the drainage engineers had been unsuccessful in convincing the residents to stop farming. Somewhat in desperation, they turned to the planning commission, since we were active in the area dealing with various land use controversies and had even held several public hearings in the area involving zoning matters. The director of the S&WB turned to the city planning director, who in turn turned to me. Mr. Katner, who knew I was somewhat familiar with the area from my work on the capital budget, told me (I was probably twenty-six or twenty-seven at the time) to go to the community, explain the issue, and persuade them to stop a practice they had historically used in their native Vietnam for generations. No problem.

I located one of the Catholic priests who administered to the community and was Vietnamese, met with him to explain the problem, and asked if he could call a community meeting where I could address the issue. I was sure that once the community clearly understood the dangers associated with farming in the canals, they would stop the practice. The priest was skeptical but agreed to call a meeting.

One evening, I went out to a community hall in New Orleans East, confident I could resolve the situation. There were maybe one hundred or so members of the community present, and they all sat on chairs toward the front of the hall, where the priest and I sat at a long table. I was wearing a suit and tie while everyone else was in street clothes or had farm overalls on. They sat very quietly, and it was obvious that the priest commanded great respect in the community as they gave him their full attention whenever he spoke. As the audience spoke little English and I obviously spoke no Vietnamese, the priest would have to translate.

The priest called the meeting to order, introduced me, and explained that I had come to talk about the community's farming practices in the drainage canals. I got up to speak, thanked everyone for coming, and launched into an explanation of the function of the drainage canals and why farming on their banks was dangerous and not permitted by the S&WB. I spoke slowly so the priest could translate. Everyone was extremely attentive and focused on every word the priest said.

Since the translation went slowly, I spoke for almost half an hour. When I was finished, I asked if there were any questions. No one spoke or held up their hand. The priest thanked everyone for coming, adjourned the meeting, and told me I was invited to eat with the community, which was having what amounted to a church social following the formal meeting.

While I declined the dinner invitation, I asked the priest how he thought my presentation went and whether the community understood the dangers of canal farming and would stop the practice. He looked at me for a moment and said, "They have no idea what you're talking about! They've practiced farming in ditches and drainage canals for thousands of years. Their parents farmed this way, their grandparents, their great-grandparents and relatives as far back as anyone can remember. They understand that when it begins to rain, they and their animals get out of the canals, wait for the rain to stop and the water to recede, and then resume their activities. They think you are a nice young man who doesn't have the first idea about their culture, their farming practices, or how to manage the canal situation. They have no intention of changing their practices, but they hope you will come, eat with them, and enjoy the rest of your evening."

I was stunned, but as I contemplated what the priest had said, I realized that the cultural divide between them and me was huge and was not going to be bridged by one presentation at a community meeting. Who did I think I was, telling them how to live their lives and questioning ancient agricultural practices that had served them well through the generations? How naïve I was! But I was also incredibly impressed at how attentive and courteous they were, even if they couldn't understand the points I was attempting to make. It was a lesson in the importance of understanding the culture of the people we planners were attempting to help—a lesson I tried to keep in mind through the years.

The next day, I met with my boss and told him about my presentation and the reaction of the community. He asked me if I thought they would cease the canal farming practice. I said absolutely not. He didn't ask me for a further explanation but called the S&WB director, told him we had a meeting with the community and delivered the message, and wished him the best of luck.

Full of Myself

The following story is adapted from a chapter I wrote in 1996 for the book Planners on Planning, *edited by Bruce McClendon and Anthony J. Catanese.*

I was fortunate that the planning commission director always allowed his junior planners the opportunity to appear before the city council to present the recommendations of the staff and the planning commission. This, of course, carried the risk that inexperienced staff could bungle the presentation or be unable to answer questions raised by the council. But Harold Katner, the planning director, was willing to take that risk to let his planners gain experience appearing before political bodies. This is where I found myself in the early 1970s.

There was an important issue regarding development in the historic French Quarter, and the planning staff had made a recommendation on the action the city council should take. The planning commission agreed with the staff, and the recommendation was sent to the council, who scheduled a time for a presentation on the issue. I was designated to make the presentation, and since this was only the second or third time I had appeared before the council, I prepared my testimony thoroughly. When the issue came up on their docket, I took my place in front of the council chambers directly in front of the seven councilmen and women. The council clerk called the matter, and I began my spiel.

I was determined to be sure that my presentation covered all the circumstances surrounding the issue and that the council could understand the rationale behind our recommendation. The longer I spoke, the more impressed I became with the compelling nature of my presentation. I was really into it and was about two-thirds of the way through my prepared remarks when I noticed that the councilman who represented the French Quarter (whose position on the matter was crucial in influencing the votes of the other council members) could hardly be seen in his chair. In fact, he was leaning way back in his chair so that just his face was barely visible above the dais, and his eyes were closed!

Clarence Dupuy Jr. was the councilman, and he was widely regarded as intelligent and shrewd but unorthodox and somewhat of a free spirit. He had represented the area since the early 1960s and had seen his share of controversial issues and members of the planning staff making presentations. He was not about to get upset at anything that occurred.

As I spoke, I became angrier and angrier that the councilman appeared to be asleep during my presentation, and when I couldn't take it any longer, I departed from my prepared text and said in righteous indignation, "Councilman Dupuy, I am making an important presentation about a matter that affects your district, and not only are you not paying attention, but you are sleeping!" My boss, who was listening on the radio in his office, jumped up and tried to get to the council chamber to apologize for my outburst, but he didn't make it in time. Meanwhile, I was feeling pretty smug about myself for demanding the attention I felt the matter deserved—until the council chambers went absolutely quiet and I knew immediately that I had screwed up. Councilman Dupuy was a senior councilman, very influential and certainly not used to being addressed in this matter, much less by a twentysomething all full of himself.

Slowly, the councilman raised his eyes. Without moving from his chair, he took a microphone and, with crystal clarity, said, "Son, I may be sleeping from the neck down, but I'm wide awake from the neck up!" The entire audience in the chamber, including the other city council members, erupted in howls of laughter. At first, I was shocked and embarrassed, but as the laughter went on, I realized that what was so important to me simply was not to the councilman. Another hard lesson learned! Pretty soon, I started laughing along and sat back to contemplate the experience. After he put me in my place, I got along fine with Councilman Dupuy until he retired in 1976.

Armstrong Park and Lawrence Halprin

In the 1950s and early '60s, many cities adopted plans for their major public facilities that attempted to group similar uses together to create complexes, which planners thought would provide synergy among facilities while making it easier for the public to use them. In New Orleans, we adopted plans that grouped police and court facilities in a particular area and built a police headquarters, district attorney offices, and municipal and traffic court buildings as well as utilizing an older criminal court building. We also created a municipal complex in the Central Business District, known as the CBD, which included a city hall, juvenile court, and a state office building. Next to the municipal complex, the city and state placed the Louisiana Supreme Court and grouped various health facilities around one of the country's great public hospitals, Charity Hospital, which not only served the entire community but also became a training ground for doctors and other medical staff.

The city also created a cultural complex centered on a historic municipal auditorium that held a variety of community events and was the location for a great variety of Mardi Gras balls and other activities. Unfortunately, the Municipal Auditorium was built in the middle of a very old and historic neighborhood called Treme. Treme was originally built as a sort of "suburban" neighborhood adjacent to the French Quarter, much like the Marigny and Bywater areas. A working-class area, Treme is arguably the oldest African American neighborhood in the United States and is a center of African American culture and musical heritage. Its long history dates from the eighteenth century, when Treme emerged as a home for free people of color, through the 1950s and '60s, when it was the home of numerous civil rights efforts. Congo Square, located in the southern corner of the Treme neighborhood, was an area where both enslaved and free people of color gathered to celebrate their heritage. Suffice it to say, it is one of the most important neighborhoods in the city and the country.

The proposed "cultural center," as envisioned by the city in the 1950s, was to contain an opera house, a science center, and even a planetarium. However, to build these cultural buildings around the Municipal Auditorium (which was built in the 1930s), many houses and businesses would have to be removed. In the early 1960s, the city, evidencing a spectacular lack of understanding of the importance of the Treme neighborhood, embarked on an urban renewal program to condemn and remove hundreds of historic properties under the guise of slum clearance.

However, after the area was cleared and a theater/opera house was built, the city ran out of money to build the other contemplated cultural facilities. A growing nationwide understanding of the destructive nature of many urban renewal programs, often called "Negro removal programs," also rallied people in New Orleans to stop any further demolition in Treme. While the halting of demolition saved what remained of the neighborhood, the project left in its wake dozens of vacant squares of ground surrounding the Municipal Auditorium and the theater.

In 1970, Maurice "Moon" Landrieu was elected mayor with significant Black support, and he was determined to do something to make amends for the damage done to the fabric of the historic Treme neighborhood. Following the death of Louis Armstrong in 1971, Mayor Landrieu appointed a committee to recommend a suitable memorial to the jazz great. The committee recommended that the now-vacant land in the Treme neighborhood surrounding the Auditorium be dedicated as a park, which would celebrate all of New Orleans's rich cultural traditions: Armstrong Park. But exactly what type of park? The mayor and Charles Ferguson, the editor of the local newspaper, visited Tivoli Gardens in Copenhagen at the suggestion of Robin Riley, a local architect, who eventually came to be the chief staff architect for the proposed park. The concept of a family attraction that would include music venues, eateries, and retail establishments while at the same time helping to broaden the city's tourist attractions beyond just the French Quarter appealed to the mayor. Landrieu was now faced with the question of how to go about creating the park.

With that as background, here is the story.

The mayor tasked architect Robin Riley with providing staff support for the park and appointed a "Client Committee" to recommend a consultant to prepare specific plans for the project. The committee included local architects Albert Saputo and Tim

Favrot (both members of the city planning commission); Leon Irwin, a local businessman; Winston Lill, Landrieu's director of public relations; and editor Charles Ferguson. In addition, John Chrestia, an architect in the mayor's office; myself, from the planning commission; and architect Riley were placed on the committee to provide staff support.

Almost from the very beginning, the name of Lawrence Halperin, an internationally known landscape architect, surfaced as the primary candidate to design the park. Halperin, who at the time was effectively the landscape architect de jour, had worked on the Seattle World's Fair and Ghirardelli Square in San Francisco. Along with Angela Danadjieva of his staff, Halperin would soon come to design Freeway Park, also in Seattle. Halperin's office was in San Francisco, and members of the Client Committee decided to go to the West Coast to interview Halperin and, hopefully, get comfortable with recommending him to the mayor.

Committee members Saputo, Favrot, Chrestia, Riley, and I made plans to travel to the Bay Area. Arthur Davis, another local architect, also accompanied us at the behest of the mayor. I was very excited to go on my first city-sponsored trip with all these very prominent architects, not only to meet with a legendary landscapc architect but also because I had never been to San Francisco. Of course, I was familiar with the city's famous reputation as a hotbed of Vietnam War resistance and as the center of the counterculture movement of the '60s and '70s. San Francisco's Haight-Ashbury neighborhood was made famous by the hippie movement and was the home of Janis Joplin, the Grateful Dead, experimental drug use, and a conglomeration of cults and religious organizations. San Francisco was also undertaking innovative planning activities in its waterfront, downtown, and neighborhoods. The combination of all these happenings made the trip thrilling for a young planner.

We flew to San Francisco on a Thursday and planned to have dinner that night and visit Halperin's office on Friday. The trip did not start well. The airline lost Tim Favot's luggage, and Tim, who had a few cocktails on the nearly five-hour flight out to the West Coast, was very unhappy and let loose with an expletive-filled rant in the airport—by which I mean he cut loose to the point where the rest of us tried to pretend we didn't know him. Finally, we persuaded Tim to go with us to the Hyatt Hotel where we were staying, and the airline promised to deliver his luggage to the hotel when they found it. That night, we ate at a fine restaurant; Tim's luggage still had not arrived.

In the morning, we set out for Halperin's office, which was in an old warehouse near the bay. Having your creative offices in an old warehouse was cutting-edge in those days and probably just another example of how San Francisco was leading the way in planning, architecture, and landscape architecture. We arrived around lunchtime and proceeded up to the building. We knocked, but no one answered. We rang the bell, but no one came to the door. We began to worry that somehow we'd gotten the arrangements for the meeting wrong and no one was home. Finally, one of us opened the front door, and we went inside.

There was no one there! There were drafting tables everywhere (it was the era before computer-aided drafting) and design drawings on the walls, the tables, and even on the floor. It was a two-story affair with conference rooms and offices mostly on the second floor. But there was nobody home. We walked around the design studio admiring the work in progress until we noticed a large outdoor patio where lots of people were milling around. Everyone was in casual dress, and everyone seemed to be smoking weed or some other substance. There were sandals, T-shirts, and headbands wherever you looked (on a Friday afternoon at lunchtime!): the epitome of San Francisco creative culture. We stood out in our suits and sport coats. The older architects in our group looked appalled that this was the team we were thinking of hiring to do the serious work of designing Armstrong Park.

One of the staff broke away from the milieu and asked if he could help us. We said we were from New Orleans and we were here to meet with Mr. Halperin and his staff. We were invited to participate in the afternoon's festivities while he went to fetch the famous landscape architect.

After a few minutes, Halperin descended the staircase from the second floor, looking very much like he was coming down from the clouds to be with us. Truth be told, he looked like a homeless man: sandals, argyle socks, open shirt, casual pants, smoking something we could only guess at. It was West Coast counterculture meets old-school Southern gentlemen (even me). Halperin showed us around the design lab and then to a conference room, where some of his staff described their design process and Halperin expounded on how excited they were about the potential of a project in New Orleans. Although a number of the staff looked gassed, after a few hours, we left feeling like Halperin might be the creative artist we were looking for to create our own version of Tivoli Gardens. We were sure he would look more presentable to the mayor away from his home base. (When Mayor Landrieu first met Halperin, Lawrence came to his office in a cape!) I thought maybe this was the way every architectural firm in San Francisco looked but was assured by my traveling companions that that was not the case.

Before we flew home the next morning, we had dinner and discussed the interview. After dinner, Arthur Davis went off on his own adventures, and John and I went to a local bar not far from the hotel. When we entered the bar, the first thing I noticed was that a number of the patrons were policemen—drinking, and I don't mean sodas. I again thought, This is what San Francisco is all about. Here was a more freewheeling locale than even those of us from New Orleans were accustomed to.

Finally, I had to go to the restroom, so I went into the men's room—only to find small television sets directly above the urinals. The TVs were playing pornographic movies! My trip to San Francisco was complete.

A Lesson in Ethics

After graduate school, I managed to keep up with only one of my classmates: Rob Lamb, who had a career throughout the Midwest. But one year, I met a fellow Iowa grad and classmate at a national planning conference, whom I'll call Jim. In school, Jim led a somewhat adventurous life—the opposite of the rest of us graduate students. He had a girlfriend who was older than him and lived in a penthouse in Winnetka, a ritzy suburb of Chicago. When our class went on a field trip to study planning in Chicago, he invited us to come out and see his girlfriend's penthouse—and of course he stayed with her on the field trip while the rest of us, including Pat and me, stayed in a downtown YMCA. Jim had his golf clubs in her apartment, so clearly, he was enjoying visiting Chicago on a fairly regular basis!

Jim went on to become the city planning director of a Florida city—which, like most Florida cities, was in the middle of a building boom. At the conference, we chatted awhile and then sat down to lunch. I had not kept up with Jim, so we swapped stories and brought each other up to date. Then he started to talk about the great car he had and showed me a picture of a magnificent sailboat he bought. I asked him how he could afford such luxury items on a public servant's salary. He told me that besides his salary, he had a side gig going designing subdivisions for various developers. I was taken aback. "You design subdivisions in your city for developers that then come before your planning commission for approval?" While we didn't have an ethics course in my curriculum at school, I thought this was a clear violation of the planning code of conduct. "Sure," he said, without the least bit of concern. "It works out great for everybody. If I design the subdivision, I know it will get approved, thus shortening the development process and keeping the developer from having to redesign and resubmit the plan because it didn't meet our standards. I make money to supplement my income, and the developer saves a good deal of money."

This conversation brought home the slippery slope you can be on as a public official and how important it is to carry out your responsibilities with high ethical standards—a lesson I've never forgotten.

Lagniappe: As I have gotten older, I find myself these days thinking about those days!

The World's Fair

In 1984, New Orleans held a world's fair (the Louisiana World Exposition) on eighty-two acres in its Central Business District. The fair, while a financial failure (the first and only world's fair to declare bankruptcy), revitalized the riverfront and the adjacent Warehouse District, drawing over seven million visitors in its six months of operation. Planning for the fair began in the late 1970s and picked up steam with the hiring of an experienced fair manager, Petr Spurney. I became the city's planning director in the early '80s and was intimately involved in the planning and permitting of the event, which dominated the city's attention for almost half a decade. The fair site was a conglomeration of private property in the Warehouse District and public land (mainly streets) and property on the riverfront. In hindsight, putting together the site was a monumental task, involving convincing numerous property owners to give up their property for almost two years so it could be converted into exhibits, restaurants, gift shops, rides, and other attractions. As the theme of the fair, World of Rivers, involved water, the Port of New Orleans was persuaded to give up its riverfront wharves and the normal river commercial activities on those wharves and in the adjacent warehouse area.

The Warehouse District buildings made up the bulk of the fair's structures. This area was originally developed in the nineteenth century to support the movement of goods passing in and out of the port. Most of the buildings were two and three stories, although there were several multistory warehouses interspersed throughout the district. The buildings were used for storage of numerous types of maritime supplies and housed machine shops, traders' offices, printers, and a few bars and restaurants that catered to longshoremen and industrial workers. The area then can best be described as a nineteenth-century version of an industrial park. Today, industrial parks are usually located in suburban areas where large single-story buildings can be built and where there is easy access to railroads, highways, and even airports. There were many discussions among city officials about whether the industrial businesses could survive their temporary conversion into fair uses or whether the coming of the fair signaled the demise of warehouse uses and the businesses' conversion into nonmaritime uses such as hotels, restaurants, art galleries, and other service businesses. The owners of the properties and their industrial tenants were very concerned but saw the fair movement as something of an unstoppable force.

The early planning for the fair focused on getting property owners to agree to temporarily turn over their property to the Fair Corporation. Individual property owners and tenants were contacted by the corporation, which promised certain property improvements in return for use of the land and buildings.

One day, I received a call from the owner of a warehouse in the middle of the fair site. He had been visited by representatives of the fair about the use of his property and was very concerned that the city, which was all in support of the project, did not understand his business or how it would be damaged by the construction and six-month operation of the event. He urgently wanted someone in authority to visit so he could explain the nature of his business and how it would be impacted. I told him I would come with a few staff and visit his operation.

On a designated day, several of us, including Lee Madere, who was the city's chief economist and a fierce advocate for the industrial uses in the Warehouse District, drove down from city hall to the business, which was indeed smack in the center of the fair site. The owner had a two-story building that took up most of a city block. When we entered the building, he greeted us warmly and led us through the office, where five or six employees were busy answering phones and taking orders for the business product, which we were told was oil field pipe. We entered the main warehouse area, which was full of different varieties and sizes of pipe, all of which were used in the oil production industry. Pipe came in by ship and then was marshalled in the warehouse to be loaded onto trucks and moved to production locations mainly in Louisiana and Texas. Obviously, the business depended on access to the port and the ease of truck access to the warehouse. The fair would displace all this activity for at least the two years the property was needed for the event. It was not possible to permit normal operations with the building inside the fenced area of the fair.

As we walked through the main portion of the warehouse, which consisted of rack after rack and row after row of long portions of metal pipe of various sizes, the owner talked about how the pipe was used and how often he had deliveries, his relationship to the port, and how dependent he was on being able to get trucks into his facility so he could load and ship the pipe to its various destinations. It was clear to me and probably to the owner that the fair was going to be the end of his business in the Central Business District and that he would need to permanently relocate to a modern industrial park or at least someplace where an industrial use could thrive utilizing modern production and storage methods and technology. Nevertheless, he was making his pitch to try to stay in the present location.

After walking us through the ground floor of the warehouse, he invited us to go to the second floor. While it seemed to me that when you'd seen one floor of pipe storage, you'd seen it all, we wanted to demonstrate our interest in hearing about all aspects of his business, so we got on a freight elevator and went up one flight to the building's second floor. More pipe. Lots and lots of pipe. But then we came to a door, and the owner invited us to come inside what was basically a large room inside the warehouse.

The first thing I noticed once we got inside was that it contained wall-to-wall carpet, including carpeting on the walls. There was a large bar, and we were invited to have a drink; I think the owner was somewhat disappointed when we declined. He turned on a first-class stereo system, and we sat down in very comfortable chairs flanking a sofa. He then explained the purpose of the room.

"I have a lot of customers who come into town from elsewhere in Louisiana and especially from Texas. The buyers who come to inspect and order my pipe expect a certain level of entertainment when they come to town, and most don't want to make a night of it in the French Quarter. So after they have dinner, I invite them back to my building for an evening's entertainment that is totally safe, secure, and discreet." You can see where this is going! "I have everything here they would want, and they can even sleep it off here if they have too much fun out on the town. We have parties and music and dancing and a lot of fun." I'm sure you do, I thought. Then we noticed that there were a few other doors, which obviously led to other rooms off the main room.

It was clear by now that the warehouse also housed other functions besides the storage of pipe. The owner had a good thing going: a thriving business that not only was ideally located near the river wharves with easy access to a good roadway network but was also near the French Quarter—where his customers liked to spend part of their evening while he made sure they enjoyed the rest of their stay in the city. He kept emphasizing to us the importance of entertaining his customers and that this was a service his competitors could not offer.

We thanked the owner for his hospitality and told him we would be sure to consider his business needs as planning for the fair moved forward. We also told him we did not think his business could continue during the run of the fair and that it would be up to him to make the best deal he could with the Fair Corporation and plan on moving his operation to a more modern location. He thanked us for coming, appreciative that at least he'd had the chance to make his case.

We wondered how many other businesses currently operating in the fair site had "unique" parts of their operation that benefited from their location near the French Quarter. After the fair ended, the pipe operation permanently relocated, and the building was repurposed for an entertainment use.

The Lengths We Will Go To

Military bases are a major driver of economic activity in many communities, and most communities will go to almost any extreme to secure a base location or a base expansion. Such was the case in Louisiana in the early 1980s when the U.S. Navy launched a program called Homeporting. The Homeporting program was conceived during the administration of President Ronald Reagan as a means to complicate Soviet missile targeting by dispersing the navy's fleet among a number of different ports so as not to group those military assets in one location (think Pearl Harbor). This was important because the navy anticipated expanding the fleet and was looking to distribute the ships in the least vulnerable manner. Along the Gulf Coast, several potential sites were proposed to hold a variety of ships in the fleet, including Mobile, Pascagoula, Pensacola, Galveston, and Ingleside in Texas. In Louisiana, Lake Charles was identified as a potential site in 1985, and New Orleans made its own pitch for a ship to be located along the Mississippi River in St. Bernard Parish.

As part of the process of making a final selection, the navy sent teams to visit various potential sites to evaluate whether they met a variety of criteria it had established as necessary for a home port. Having even one major naval vessel located in your community meant hundreds if not thousands of jobs, including the navy's shipboard personnel, staffing for the maintenance and supplying of the ships, security for the home port area, and, of course, jobs in the private sector in the restaurant, entertainment, and hotel industries.

New Orleans had put forth its proposal and was anxious to see what other proposed locations were doing to advocate for their sites—in effect, scoping out the competition. The city knew that Lake Charles was likely to be our biggest competitor, so a group of city employees decided to pay a day visit to Lake Charles to evaluate their efforts.

We were hosted by the local chamber of commerce, which was going all out to recruit the navy. Members told us that they had utilized all the traditional tools of economic developers, including a very comprehensive proposal that outlined the area's assets, such as recreational opportunities, easy access to transportation facilities, the low cost of housing, and so on. However, they went above and beyond the traditional economic development pitch to include initiatives we never thought of.

The Lake Charles Chamber of Commerce knew that the visit by the navy's team would make or break their efforts to secure a ship. The navy's preliminary analysis had identified Lake Charles as, potentially, a good location for a major supply vessel and supporting infrastructure, and a final selection of their site would be a huge economic boon for the area. The chamber and the city were determined to leave no stone unturned to impress the navy on their visit.

These are some of the steps the Lake Charles officials told us they took to make their community seem as desirable as possible to the navy team. While touring the community with the navy personnel, they took them to a local restaurant so they could sample the great food southern Louisiana is known for. Everybody does that. However, the Lake Charles officials had special menus printed for the restaurant that contained much lower prices for the food offerings than was normally the case, to give the impression that local restaurants were affordable for the average sailor. Similarly, when they drove the navy around to look at housing, they made sure to visit areas where the prices were modest, as opposed to areas along the Gulf Coast that had higher price points.

But perhaps the most creative strategy they told us about involved the hotel where the navy's inspection team was staying. The Hilton Hotel in downtown Lake Charles was the selected location, and the rate charged was significantly below the normal market rate. Not only that, officials recruited a number of coeds from area universities to be out by the pool deck whenever the navy's team was at the hotel.

When you are desperate, you will go to almost any length. Unfortunately for Lake Charles, as well as other home port candidate cities along the Gulf Coast, by the early 1990s, the program had been dropped after the Base Realignment and Closure Commission recommended that it be canceled. Still, you have to hand it to Lake Charles for the creativity they showed in their efforts to recruit the navy.

The Odd Fellows Cemetery

Blaise Carriere was as fine a public servant as I have ever known. Blaise, who was a civil engineer, worked with the state highway department as a bridge engineer before coming to the attention of Maurice "Moon" Landrieu, who appointed him director of the City Streets Department when he was elected mayor in 1970. In his position, Blaise was concerned with all aspects of building and repairing streets, but he had a particular passion for trying to make the existing street system function more efficiently. In his heart, I think Blaise was basically a traffic engineer. Like many engineers, he was consumed with the engineering aspect of his job—and determined to make streets safer and more efficient while being somewhat unaware of the collateral damage that sometimes occurs with public improvements.

After I had been with the planning commission for several years, when I was in my role as head of the capital budget section, Harold Katner, the planning director, asked me to go to a meeting with him in the office of the chief administrative officer (CAO), Richard Kernion. Kernion, who was the brother-in-law of the mayor, held the most important position in city government, something like a city manager. All departments reported to him, and he was responsible for all aspects of budgeting and construction. He was a big deal, and meetings with him were usually limited to department heads and other important officials. So I was excited to be invited to a meeting where he would be in attendance. Katner told me that Blaise Carriere would also be in the meeting, which made me doubly excited to be with a department director, the planning director, and the CAO.

Katner and I went to the CAO's office, where Blaise was busy setting up an easel with a presentation board attached. I soon learned that the meeting concerned Blaise's proposal for a street improvement at the intersection of City Park Avenue and Canal Boulevard in the Mid-City section of New Orleans. I knew this intersection to be where Canal Boulevard took a "jog" in order to go around the Odd Fellows Cemetery and then continue toward the lake. The jog was necessary because the continuation of Canal Boulevard toward the lake did not align directly with Canal Street coming up from the Central Business District. This misalignment required lake-bound traffic to make a right turn at City Park Avenue and then a quick left turn back onto Canal Boulevard. The opposite was true traveling south (or river-bound, in New Orleans speak) from Canal Boulevard to reconnect to Canal Street. This jog required a complicated signal system and, at peak travel times, could hold up traffic—and in extreme circumstances, it could be confusing to drivers, causing accidents. Blaise hated the intersection. The problem with having a smooth, continuous Canal Street running from the river to the lake was the Odd Fellows Cemetery. To smooth out Canal Street, a portion of the cemetery would have to be acquired, the bodies disinterred, and a new street section constructed.

The Odd Fellows Cemetery opened in 1849 and is one of several historic cemeteries in New Orleans. It is the oldest fraternal cemetery in the city and was constructed as a burial place for members of the Odd Fellows fraternity. The Independent Order of Odd Fellows is a nonpolitical, nonsectarian international fraternal order founded in the United States in 1819. The Odd Fellows do good deeds, particularly visiting the sick and distressed and burying the dead. The latter task was very important during yellow fever epidemics, when the cemetery was opened to those who succumbed to the disease. The cemetery is now closed to the public and is listed on the National Register of Historic Places.

Once everyone had settled into the CAO's office, Kernion said the purpose of the meeting was for Blaise to present his proposal to straighten out the alignment of Canal Street and eliminate any traffic hazards the current intersection presented. Blaise then launched into his reasons for wanting to "modernize" the intersection and the method he was recommending for accomplishing the realignment. A portion of the cemetery, he told us, would have to be demolished to make way for the roadway improvements. That meant acquiring part of the over-one-hundred-year-old cemetery, disinterring the remains of somewhere between fifty and one hundred people, finding a suitable place to rebury them, demolishing or moving the designated tombs, constructing a new roadway segment linking Canal Street directly with Canal Boulevard, and reconfiguring the traffic control systems and signage. He did not have a figure for the estimated cost of the project because he didn't know the cost of acquiring the property, which could range widely if the city had to expropriate it.

When Blaise finished his presentation, there was a brief period of silence before Mr. Kernion spoke. He looked at the three of us and said, "Let me see if I understand what is being proposed." At this point, I didn't know if Harold Katner was in support of the scheme or not. He had not said a word, pro or con. I just kept my mouth shut. "You want me to go to the mayor and the city council and tell them we want to expropriate a large part of a historic cemetery in this Catholic city from the Odd Fellows fraternity, an organization known for its good deeds, relocate the graves of yellow fever victims, demolish the part of the cemetery we acquire, and build a roadway segment for the purpose of straightening out Canal Street. Is that about the size of it?"

Blaise, looking the part of the righteous engineer proposing a much-needed improvement the merits of which were overwhelming, said, "That's correct."

There was another moment of silence, and then Mr. Kernion, who was a very street-savvy politician in addition to being the CAO, looked around the room and said, "Get the f— out of my office! Are you crazy? Even if this project was urgently needed, which it isn't, the Odd Fellows are not going to give us this property. We would have to try and expropriate it from a well-respected organization that voluntarily accepted the dead from yellow fever epidemics! What is the matter with you?"

With that lesson in politics, he ushered us out of his office, where Blaise's proposal died that day. The street still jogs, and the cemetery remains undisturbed.

A Bathroom Story

Every public servant will tell you that there are a few tasks that must be accomplished no matter what obstacles you face. For a manager of a public park, those include picking up the trash, cutting the grass, and shoveling the snow. You must make sure no one steals your money through theft, fraud, or careless accounting. And you must make sure your public bathrooms are always safe, clean, and working properly.

Seems easy enough—except when it's not. People trash public parks during normal use, let alone during special events, when food and beverages are ubiquitous. Sometimes your grass-cutting equipment is broken, or your grass cutters get sick or go on vacation, or it rains steadily for days, which prevents you from keeping up a normal maintenance schedule. Occasionally you might have a careless or even dishonest employee who, despite all evidence to the contrary, believes they can get away with theft or fraud. But even with all that, you must keep the public bathrooms safe and clean.

In the years after Hurricane Katrina, we tried to repair our public bathrooms, and we experimented with different opening and closing hours and different maintenance schedules as well as hiring private companies versus using our own employees. Where the bathrooms were damaged in the storm, we used dollars from FEMA to repair them. Most of the bathrooms in City Park were old, many having been built more than sixty years before, and as a result, they were extremely difficult to keep clean, safe, and in good working order. One solution to this problem was to build new bathrooms where we could incorporate the latest in bathroom architectural design.

We finally decided to build a new shelter in the front of City Park near Christian Brothers School (a private school occupying park buildings under a decade-old contract), and along with that shelter, we built an adjacent building with bathrooms. The building was brick with the latest in plumbing fixtures. Users would enter a small open vestibule and go either left or right to enter the men's or the women's area. The main entrance to each set of toilets or urinals had locks so our security staff could lock off one or both rooms. The arrangement seemed to accommodate any eventuality.

One afternoon, shortly after the bathrooms had been locked for the day, our security department got a call from the New

Orleans Police Department. They had received a panicked call from a woman who claimed she was locked in our shelter's bathroom and couldn't get out. The city police asked our officers to investigate.

Several of our officers went immediately to the shelter—a little confused, since they had checked both sides of the bathroom before determining there was no one there and locking the building. When they arrived, they went first to the women's side, unlocked the building, and after announcing their presence, went inside. They again examined the room, including looking under the toilet partitions, but could find no one. Just before they were about to leave, they heard a female voice calling for help. They went to each stall and finally found a young woman standing on the toilet.

After helping her down, our officers asked how she managed to get locked in when they had previously come by and, before locking the building, looked under the partition of each stall to be certain no one was still on the toilet. She explained that she did not hear a knock or anyone calling out but knew that someone had entered the building. She'd recently had a fight with her boyfriend and was terrified that he had entered to do her harm. So she climbed up on the toilet to hide, and thus when park police looked under the partitions, they did not see anyone. After the police left the building, she was too scared to come down, so she stayed on top of the toilet for at least half an hour before she decided to call 911 since it was now dark outside and, she thought, she could have been locked in until morning—which is exactly what would have happened.

Our officers escorted her out of the restrooms and looked around the immediate vicinity to be sure no one was waiting in the darkened shelter. They then called her a cab so she could go home and called the New Orleans police to tell them the 911 call had been resolved, thus ending the mystery of how a woman could be locked inside an empty bathroom. Just another day in a public park.

The Fork in the Road

"If you don't know where you are going, you might wind up someplace else." —Yogi Berra

What do you think of when you think of Buffalo? Cold and snow, right? To be honest, that's what many of my memories of western New York are: snow pants, parkas, woolen mittens, and cold feet. It seemed like my feet were always cold. My father and most of my friends' fathers worked in factories, and most of our moms did not have full-time jobs. But I had wonderful friends and a caring family, and there always seemed to be plenty to do. The following are a few stories of my fondest memories.

The News Business

I was employed in some sort of job, from the time I was ten years old until I retired, for sixty-three years. While I primarily held full-time jobs, I also had part-time employment, including as a newspaper boy, bowling pin setter, store clerk, and graduate assistant. Everyone I knew had some type of part-time job. That's the way it was in our working-class neighborhood in Buffalo, New York.

My father was a lens polisher at the American Optical

Company, making bombsights and telescope lenses. Because of the importance of the work, he was given a critical employee exemption from the military draft. He walked miles to work, worked hard, and always brought home his paycheck, with only a Friday night at the local tavern for relaxation. In his younger days, he was an excellent bowler, bowling in many league teams and winning lots of awards. When a medical condition no longer allowed him to grip the bowling ball, he became somewhat reclusive, going to work and then straight to the bedroom.

My mother was a stay-at-home mom until she was in her late forties, when she got a job as a cafeteria worker at my elementary school, which was about ten blocks from my house. As my father became more reclusive, mom became more engaged. She learned how to drive, bought a car, stopped smoking, and became more active with her friends and our relatives. Mom handled the family finances and always kept track of how much I was making at various jobs right up through high school.

My earliest job, besides shoveling snow for a few neighbors, was delivering newspapers. When we moved to New Orleans, Pat and I were surprised to learn that there were only newspaper men or women, whereas in Buffalo, there were only newspaper boys. Perhaps the pay was so low that adults didn't find delivering the papers to be profitable in New Orleans, or maybe delivering newspapers was just beneath the working-class adults I knew. Whatever the reason, children delivered papers in Buffalo, while adults delivered the news in New Orleans.

Being in the newspaper business in Buffalo was complicated by the weather. It always seemed to me that Buffalo had only two seasons: cold and not so cold. When school started after Labor Day, it was already jacket weather—contrast that with the South, where winter seems to begin in December and last until the first of March.

I started out helping another boy with his paper route when I was ten and then got my own route in my neighborhood a few years later. I started with the morning route, which began with a truck delivering all the papers to my house at around six o'clock. While I don't remember exactly, I believe I had around one hundred homes that received the morning paper. After a while, I switched to delivering the evening news to around the same number.

When the papers arrived, I would put them in a large wagon and go from house to house delivering the news. In those days, you didn't just throw the paper on the sidewalk or the driveway as is the common practice today. You were expected to deliver the paper to the door: that is, open the screen or storm door and put the paper inside. This wasn't that difficult until the weather turned cold, which it did for seven or eight months of the year. Now, if cold weather was the only problem, it wouldn't have been that bad. But with the cold weather came snow—lots and lots of snow. Buffalo is famous for what is termed *lake effect snow*: that is, snow that comes from the west across Lake Erie and picks up volume and speed. The combination of temperatures that were routinely in the twenties and blizzard-like snow made delivering papers in the dark of winter a nightmare for a ten-year-old kid.

Postal workers have many stories about their experiences delivering the mail. So do newspaper boys. I was bitten on numerous occasions by dogs people let out to do their business early in the morning, sometimes while trying to work my way up a snow-filled driveway to put the paper in the door. Or I'd find people who locked their screen door and then got mad when you couldn't put their paper in the door. Then there was the effort to collect payment from customers. If the newspaper company gave you one hundred papers, it expected payment for all one hundred. It was up to you, the paperboy, to collect payment from the customer so as to be able to pay the company. My mother would often sit with me and help me keep track of my business by recording who paid, who owed me money, and when payment was due.

When the day came for customers to pay (which was usually a Friday), some people wouldn't come to the door. (Remember, this was way before you could pay online or even by mail. Payment was a face-to-face transaction.) Or they turned out the lights like some do on Halloween and pretended they weren't home. Or they made you stand outside in the freezing cold while they searched for the money inside their warm house. Or they told you that they didn't get the paper last Wednesday and were deducting that cost from their payment.

While I didn't make a lot of money on my paper route, I did make some spending money, which I mostly used to buy baseball trading cards. In the 1950s, the Topps Company produced major league baseball cards, often in packages, which also included bubblegum. My friends and I played endless baseball games with the cards, using dice to score runs. We played our favorite teams and players, kept records, and traded cards for hours on end. By the time I started college, I had boxes and boxes of cards, which I kept under my bed. Unfortunately, when I left home for graduate school in Iowa, my mom threw out my cards. I don't know whether my collection contained the 1952 Mickey Mantle card, which sold in 2024 for more than $12 million, but I sure would have liked to find out!

I learned a great deal about business and human nature from being a newspaper boy—skills that stood me in good stead during my career. I learned patience and diplomacy by having to deal with a wide variety of personalities, and I became pretty good at sizing people up quickly and knowing who would be paying their bill and who would take every opportunity to stiff me on Fridays. I learned that the paper company didn't care if there was a blizzard that prevented me from delivering the papers or if I couldn't collect all that was owed me. They wanted their money regardless, and excuses wouldn't be tolerated. It was my introduction to the ruthless world of capitalism.

My Most Embarrassing Moment

Have you ever been embarrassed? Of course you have—some of us many times. Dictionaries generally describe embarrassment as a feeling of self-consciousness, shame, or awkwardness. Most of us have experienced such feelings periodically through our lives. However, how many of us can remember their most embarrassing moment—the one that stands out and tops them all? I can.

I was sixteen. Several of my friends were invited by other boys from a nearby recreation center for a pickup basketball game and wanted me to come. Now, I was not then a basketball fan. (I'm even less of a fan today, but that's another story.) I loved baseball and bowling but not basketball. It didn't help that I rarely played basketball and was admittedly terrible at it. But I wanted to be with my friends, so I took our car and drove to the center. I had just gotten my license and was enjoying the sense of freedom the car provided.

I went to the center in the evening, met up with my friends Jim Maciejewski and Phil Federico, and sized up the other team. From the get-go, I had the feeling that this was a mistake. The other players were bigger, faster, and more skilled than anyone on my team, and I was the smallest player on either side. We'd barely been playing for twenty minutes when I went up for a rebound (what the heck was I doing under the basket in the first place?) and collided with I don't know how many players who were trying for the same rebound. I felt something crack in my knee and the sick feeling you get when you know something is terribly wrong with your body. I fell to the ground, grabbed my knee, and knew instantly that I wouldn't be playing any more basketball that night—or, as it turned out, ever again. I limped to the side of the gym and sat on the bench, in tremendous pain. My so-called friends called out for me to go back on the floor and to toughen up. That was not going to happen, so I told them I was finished and I was going home. When I got in the car, I realized that I was injured in my right knee and therefore would have to drive with my left leg on the gas all the way home. Try it sometime—not fun.

When I got home, the knee was badly swollen, and by the time morning came, my mother knew I had to go to the hospital. I was examined in the emergency room, and the doctor told us that my knee was badly damaged and I would need an operation. I don't remember if he told us I had torn my ACL, but as it turned out, almost fifty years later, my orthopedic surgeon confirmed that that was my injury. In 1963—which, medically speaking, was about the time of the dinosaurs—I had torn my ACL but didn't know it. Mom made all the arrangements, and the next day, I was in surgery.

When I woke from the anesthetic, my mom said the surgeon (whom I recall never meeting) told her that the operation went well and I would be in the hospital recovering for three weeks. (Today, you'd be up and out of the hospital in three days.) Neither my mother nor I understood exactly what the operation entailed or what I could expect the result to be. Almost fifty years later, I had a knee replacement operation, and the surgeon (who was head of the sports orthopedic unit at New Orleans's largest hospital) told me that I'd been walking around for all that time with a torn ACL. No wonder that for my entire adult life I couldn't run or play sports like tennis or baseball that required movement around the court or the playing field. I could walk, and that was about it.

At the time, two or three weeks in the hospital to recover from a knee operation was considered routine. I was going to miss a lot of school, which ended my career in organic chemistry. I settled into a routine at the hospital and began physical therapy.

One day, I think around ten o'clock in the morning, a couple hours after I'd taken my latest pain pill, I was lying in bed with my eyes closed, sort of whiling away the time until lunch came. Through the haze, I could hear the door to my room open, and I knew people were coming into the room. I figured it was just another blood pressure or temperature check, so I continued lying there, semi-asleep and feeling pretty good. There seemed to be quite a bit of talking, so I cracked one eye open, expecting to see a doctor, nurse, or—hopefully—lunch.

What I saw was at least half a dozen young girls who, back then, were called candy stripers: volunteers who worked under the supervision of the nursing staff. They were usually high school students who were investigating whether they wanted a career in nursing or some other medical profession, and they often shadowed the experienced staff or were doing some sort of internship. In the '60s, candy stripers were almost universally young girls. The group had gathered around my bed and was listening to a nurse. She told them they were going to learn how to give a patient a bath while in bed. Remember, I was a sixteen-year-old boy.

The nurse pulled back the sheet and then my gown so that there was nothing between me and the sky. I was frozen, unable to move. I kept my eyes closed, pretending to be asleep—as though you could be asleep while you were being manipulated and wet washcloths were being used to clean you up. I'm sure everyone, especially the girls, knew I was faking it. "Roll him over on his side. Be sure not to stretch the stiches. Take the washcloth and squeeze it before you use it so as not to get too much water on the patient. Start at the hips and go down the legs. Use the towel to dry off the parts you have washed." *OMG*. Then there was giggling and the girls talking under their breath. I prayed for the lesson to end, but it seemed like it went on forever.

And—you guessed it—I became excited. I'm sure I must have been as red as the sun as I kept my eyes closed and hoped no one would notice. But they kept on, and someone—to this day, I am hopeful it was the nurse—demonstrated how to wash my private parts. Then they started on my upper torso. All the while, I had my eyes closed as tightly as I could get them, and my lower body was at attention. They must have been thinking: *How could he possibly be asleep?*

Wait, maybe they'll think I was dead! I thought. *What if one of these girls goes to my high school? What if one of them is dating one of my friends? Maybe I could transfer to another school. Mom will understand, I know. Or maybe we could move to another city or even state. When will it end?*

I was too stunned to be embarrassed, too rigid like a corpse to see any light at the end of the tunnel. But after what seemed like days, they covered me back up and began to leave the room. I sneaked a peek and could see them all talking and laughing as they left the room. Why were they laughing? What were they laughing at? At sixteen, you don't know whether you're gifted, average, or—the worst of all worlds—substandard. As I thought about whether I would be the talk of the candy striper class or my high school, I felt exhausted and drained. Had this really happened, or was the pain pill working overtime? I believe I was flushed the entire day. Soon after, lunch came, and then, mercifully, I was taken down to physical therapy.

Many years and many other embarrassing experiences later, the candy striper episode still stands out as the single most humiliating experience in my life—hands down. Because I had my eyes closed for most of the time, I can't recall the faces of any of those girls, so I never knew as I went through the rest of high school and then college (I went to the University of Buffalo as an undergraduate, so I stayed in the city) whether any of them ever recognized me as the boy who got a bath in his bed. I will never know.

The Atomic Clock

In my senior year of high school, we were required to take physics, a subject that was not my intellectual pursuit. I never could get the hang of physics—unlike the other required sciences, like biology and chemistry. Recognizing my lack of accomplishment in this, the most basic of sciences, my guidance counselor responded by putting me in the honors physics class.

As part of the class, all honors physics students were required to participate in the county science fair, where your physics project would be in competition with hundreds of other projects from around the region. Since I could hardly grasp the theory of the lever and fulcrum, I knew I was going to be in deep trouble not only coming up with a project but also actually executing it. Fortunately, the science fair permitted partnering up with other students for a submission. I picked out one of the smartest kids in my class, whom I bowled with in a bowling league, Joe Bettinger, and offered to partner up with him. Joe (who later was the best man at my wedding) really didn't need a partner but took pity on me and agreed to take me aboard. *Wonderful*, I thought. What did he have in mind for a project?

Joe informed me that we would be building an atomic clock. Say what? I thought it would be beyond us just to build a clock, let alone an atomic clock. Even my rudimentary knowledge of physics suggested that somehow, radiation was involved, and I thought that would be dangerous. Joe was unphased at my concern. We were going to call it atomic, but our clock would be built using the principles of atomic energy without handling any radioactive materials. Thank God.

After several months of meeting at Joe's house and throwing together something resembling a clock (I had no idea what I was doing other than to do what Joe told me to do), we were ready for the fair. My main contribution was making presentation boards based on ideas and suggestions from my partner. I knew Joe had built the clock to plug into an outlet and that good old normal electricity would power our submission.

One Saturday in the spring, Joe's father drove us down to the local auditorium where the fair was being held. We walked in with our project, found our designated spot among the hundreds of exhibits, and got to work setting up. As my partner fiddled with the clock, I looked around and saw there were students who had biology projects, chemistry projects,

projects on astronomy—there were even students who made replicas of dinosaurs out of clay and created a diorama for their submission. The hall was full, and the judging of all the projects by college science teachers was beginning. When the judging began, students were expected to stand beside their projects and answer questions from the judges. Of course, everyone was looking at everyone else's project and trying to convince themselves that their effort was better than those and they were in line to win a blue ribbon. As I had no knowledge of how our clock was constructed, I was particularly terrified that I would be called on to answer some physics questions—or, better yet, asked why our project was called an atomic clock when there was nothing atomic about it.

I told Joe it was time to plug in the clock so the judges could see it running. (At least I hoped it ran.) So as maybe one thousand people milled about the exhibition hall, we launched our atomic clock. Joe plugged it in, and it immediately blew up and caught fire. (Years later, I learned that the outlet by the exhibit had both AC and DC ports; Joe plugged the clock into the DC port, causing the explosion and fire.) There was chaos all around us as parents, judges, and staff looked for a fire extinguisher to put out the fire. We stood there dumbfounded until Joe said, "Let's get out of here!" What else could we do? Carefully moving ourselves away from our charred exhibit, we made for the door, taking care not to run or acknowledge anyone else. Joe's father was outside, and we ran up to him. We had to go, we told him. The judging would take hours so there was no point hanging around.

Needless to say, our atomic clock was the talk of our physics class the next Monday. Our physics teacher, Joseph Militello, did not suffer fools gladly, and I knew information about our clock disaster must have reached him by the time our class convened. Mr. Militello, putting on a front like he didn't know what had happened, started the class by congratulating everyone for participating and then asked how the team of

Becker and Bettinger had done. Of course, everyone knew of our disaster, but Joe and I put on a brave face, explaining that all science is advanced even when experiments fail before we recounted what happened. I don't know whether our physics teacher punished Joe with a lower letter grade for our now-notorious physics project. I knew I was destined for a C in the course anyway, so it really didn't matter. I'm not sure whether our school was invited back to the fair the next year. I do know that the atomic clock was a fork in the road for me, confirming that my future career was not going to be in the field of science.

Lagniappe: When you are "over the weather," it usually means you are ready for winter to be over and spring to begin or ready for summer to be over and cooler weather to arrive. But if you are "under the weather," the expression has nothing to do with the weather but simply denotes that you aren't feeling well. Why is that? Perhaps it refers to the eighteenth-century practice of taking sailors on wooden ships belowdecks and out of the weather when they became sick. Today, you can be over the weather, under the weather, or out of the weather—very confusing!

Who's In Charge Here?

My mother was a small woman, five feet tops and slight of stature. But she was a dynamo, always on the go, knitting, baking, and preserving peaches and other fruits while holding down a job as a cook in the local public elementary school.

For the first few years after I was born, my parents rented an apartment, and they eventually purchased a small house in Buffalo on Ericson Avenue in the Bailey/Delevan section of town. It was a typical small house in an ethnic neighborhood where every child went to the public elementary school and walked or biked the few blocks from their houses to PS No. 71. This was a time when doctors came to your house if you were sick. I clearly remember Dr. Romano coming to our house when I was six and ill with pneumonia. A big Saturday consisted of baseball practice and then biking with friends several miles to the newly opened McDonald's, where you could get a hamburger, a small French fries, and a drink for thirty-five cents each.

My mother was raised Lutheran, and every Sunday, we took the bus several miles to attend Trinity Lutheran E&R (Evangelical/Reform) church for services. When Palm Sunday came, the congregation would go outside and parade around the block holding palm fronds. Even in the winter, we paraded.

When Pat and I settled in New Orleans, we found a similar pattern: a variety of neighborhoods usually oriented around cultural and religious institutions. You lived in the Lower Garden District or Uptown near several universities or in the Bywater or Marigny. I was also surprised to learn that many people grew up in the French Quarter, which Northerners always thought was all about Bourbon Street, where everyone was a tourist. Today, there is a constant tension between the economic benefits of tourism in the Quarter and its historical function as a neighborhood where locals live. Of course, Buffalo was not a tourist destination, unless you decided to visit Niagara Falls.

When I was in eighth grade, my mom bought her first car and imposed on relatives to teach her how to drive. She took my cousin and me to New York City to see the sights, and we stayed at a hotel that catered to wrestlers. She thought that was such a hoot and talked about it for years.

My mother was kind, generous, and generally mild-mannered. It took a lot for her to get upset. I was a junior in high school before I discovered just how far she could be pushed. Do you remember when you were in high school and just coming into your own? I learned to drive, started dating a few girls, played American Legion baseball, and graduated from delivering newspapers to a part-time job at Twin Fair, an all-purpose store similar to Target. To put it bluntly, I was in full high school mode.

One day, I came home from school and found my mother in the kitchen preparing dinner. I sat down at the kitchen table, which was generally the center of activity, and asked in a snarky way when we were going to have dinner. I'm pretty sure I was rude. Mom replied, "In an hour or so," and I made some disparaging remark. Then I was asked to take out the garbage. It was winter, so it was cold, and there was a lot of snow on the ground, which meant I had to put back on my winter coat and boots, which I'd just taken off to come inside. I didn't like it and complained loudly that I was always being asked to do some chore. My mother ignored me, but in hindsight, I now realize she was getting aggravated. At the time, I was oblivious to her feelings and continued sulking and generally acting like a spoiled brat. Then she asked me to get a specific spice from the spice cabinet, which was next to the stove. I was already five foot seven and towered over my small mother, so it was easy for me to get the spice she asked for. But again, I said something stupid and rude.

Suddenly, my mother spun around, grabbed a frying pan that was sitting on the stove, and hit me on the side of my head with it. For a small woman, she had quite an arm. The force of the blow stunned me and knocked me down, and I went sprawling on the floor. My mother walked over, stood over me with the pan in her hand, and said, "Robert"—my mother never called me Robert unless I was in deep trouble—"don't you ever talk to me like that again!" I stared at her from the floor in pain and disbelief, but you know what? I never again talked back to her. Lesson delivered.

My Second Most Embarrassing Moment

So many embarrassing moments, so difficult to pick. It seems to me that those moments often come when you are younger and before you've started to make your way in the world. Perhaps it's because you are so naïve or so inexperienced that you naturally stumble into them. Or perhaps when you get older, you don't want to admit to being humiliated. But when you're younger, those moments always seem to involve girls (or boys, if the shoe fits).

When I was a junior at the University of Buffalo—make it 1968—my friend Gary Belcher, who had a regular girlfriend, told me he was taking her to a formal dance. "Fine," I said. "I hope you have a great time." But there was a problem. Gary's girl wouldn't go to the prom unless her roommate also went, but she didn't have a date, and Gary wanted me to be that date. I did not have a regular girlfriend and was somewhat shy. I had never been on a blind date, and the thought of taking a girl I had never met to a dance didn't seem too attractive to me.

But Gary insisted, and finally, I agreed to double date with him and his girl. Almost from the beginning, I felt this was a bad idea, but I had made the commitment and was going to follow through. Gary made it a little easier by saying that he would drive. Now, he had a red Mustang, and I thought that would make a good impression not only on my date but also on everyone when we drove up to the dance.

The girls were attending Buffalo State Community College, which was commonly known as Buff State and was primarily a college for future teachers. It also had a reputation for having some of the prettiest girls in the city. Maybe this wouldn't be so bad after all.

When prom night came, Gary picked me up at my house. We both had tuxedos and corsages for the girls. I was incredibly nervous for my first blind date, but Gary had assured me that his girl told him her roommate was attractive and very personable. We drove out to the campus and up to their dormitory and went inside, and Gary called his date from the lobby to let them know we had arrived.

They came down the stairs. *Oh my goodness* was my first reaction. My date was not just attractive; she was gorgeous! She was at least six feet tall in her stocking feet, while I am five foot seven and a half on my best day. She was wearing heels, which probably made her six three, and she towered over me. She was perfectly made up and honestly looked like some statuesque movie star. Me, I looked like I was in high school and was the kid brother accompanying his older sister to the dance. The blood drained out of my face, and I could hardly say hello.

We went out to Gary's car, and I got in the back seat. I tried to push off the floor with my feet to appear taller sitting next to her. It didn't work. I'm sure she was appalled that her date was so short and immature looking. When we got to the dance, it got worse. When a slow dance came, I barely came up to her chest! She tried to make the best of a bad situation by taking off her heels and only dancing the fast dances so we didn't have to be close together—which, of course, only emphasized the great difference in our heights. As the evening dragged on, I prayed for an end to the embarrassment, as I'm sure she did as well. Even today, I get red-faced just thinking about the disaster.

We didn't go out after the dance was over. I'm sure my date told her girlfriend that she wanted the evening to end as soon as possible, and we dropped them off at the dorm and went home. Gary was disappointed; he'd hoped for a better end to the evening. He later let me know that his date told him her roommate didn't want to be called for any future get-togethers, and that was my first and last experience blind dating—another fork in the road. I learned it was better to spend some lonely nights than to trust your friends to recommend companions.

The Reunion

No set of stories would be complete without a recounting of that most American of traditions: the high school reunion. Since my wife, Pat, and I have returned to Buffalo only on a very infrequent basis, I was excited to get word in 2015 that my high school was having a fiftieth-year reunion of the graduating class of 1965. (Who even keeps track of things like that?) One of my friends had given the organizers my address, and they sent a notice describing all the activities that would take place over the designated weekend, including a dance on Friday night and a class barbecue on Saturday. I flew to Buffalo on a Thursday afternoon and had dinner at a downtown restaurant with several of the guys who stood in my wedding, several of whom were going to the reunion. Friday was spent visiting relatives and having dinner with my favorite cousin, so amid all those activities, I skipped the dance.

The main event of the weekend was the barbecue, held at a suburban location that had large grounds where they catered parties, weddings, and events like the reunion. The venue had a large parking lot adjacent to the picnic grounds where tables and chairs were set up, so it was easy to get to the buffet line. I had a yearbook with me that I'd purchased online as my original book was lost during Hurricane Katrina. I quickly met several of my classmates, who signed my book as I signed theirs, and then roamed the grounds looking for others. After fifty years, it was hard to identify people, so the organizers had made large badges with our name and our high school picture to make connecting easier. Of course, there was also a table with pictures of members of the class who had passed away, a sobering reminder of the toll fifty years can take.

During the afternoon, several awards were given out in various categories, such as the first person to retire and the classmate who traveled farthest to get to the gathering. (I thought I might win coming from New Orleans, but someone from Hawaii took the prize.) I went through the buffet line and settled in at a large table with my friends and classmates Bob Wunsch and Gary Belcher and a few others whom I hadn't immediately recognized. We were going through the yearbook and reminiscing about various classmates and teachers, particularly laughing about the future occupations and colleges we'd all put by our pictures fifty years ago. I had said I was going to become a teacher and go to the University of Buffalo. Other occupations that were listed included chemist, nurse, architect, bookkeeper, teacher, secretary, electrician, and many more. Some of those predictions had come true, like teacher and nurse, but many more, like mine, had not.

While we were eating, a yellow Corvette drove into the parking lot close to where our table was located, and a man and a woman got out. Everyone at the table couldn't help noticing that the woman was considerably younger than the man and extremely attractive. After a short time, the couple, who had gotten their food, came over to our table as we had extra seats available and sat down. The man was one of our classmates. Now, every high school class at that time had its share of boys who were, let's say, on the rough side and who often came to class in boots and motorcycle chains. You know—the kind of guy you went to the other side of the hallway to avoid lest you accidently bump into him and he knock your lights out. Alan (that's what I'll call him) was that kind of guy. We all knew that Alan would never amount to anything, and he reinforced our opinion by writing in the yearbook that he wanted to become an auto mechanic. We were all going to college, but Alan was going to be an auto mechanic.

However, there he was in a yellow Corvette with a woman on his arm who looked like she'd just flown in from Hollywood. My curiosity was overwhelming, and since I was sitting close to him, I inquired as innocently as I could, "Well, Alan, what have you been doing with yourself these last fifty years?" (What else can you open with when you haven't seen or heard from someone since you graduated high school?) Alan said, "When I left high school, I went to work as an auto mechanic at a small gas station in Buffalo." This was still a time when an independent garage could fix your broken car—as opposed to today, when you're forced to go to a dealership for anything major.

"I worked there for a couple of years," Alan went on, "and

then the owner was going to sell the business, so I put together some money and bought the garage. A couple of years later, another garage opportunity opened up, and I bought that as well. A few more years went by, and another opportunity came along, and today I'm kind of semiretired, with my staff running my businesses." Really! The guy we all thought would never amount to anything had become a successful businessman, and if the Corvette was any indication, he was worth a lot more money than any of my classmates. Plus, there was his beautiful and much younger companion. So much for thinking that anyone who didn't go to college wouldn't be successful.

Finally, I asked Alan, "What do you do with yourself now that you're semiretired?" He looked at me and said, "Now my life revolves around fast cars and fast women!"

Graduate School

"The road to success is always under construction" —Lily Tomlin

When I began my senior year at the University of Buffalo, I began to think about what I was going to do after graduation. I quickly realized that as a history major, my choices were going to be teacher or department manager at Sears. I began looking through graduate school catalogues to see what interested me, took the GRE, and settled on programs in city planning or city management. I confess I was not too clear about the difference between the programs, but I began applying to various ones. I spoke with the head of the University of Iowa program, James Harris, as well as Professors Barbara Bailey, who taught design classes, and Dave Raney, who taught social planning, and liked them immediately. I was accepted to several programs, but the two-year Iowa program in city planning seemed most exciting, and they offered the most financial assistance, so I settled on it—even though I did not know exactly where Iowa was or how to get there. So in 1969, I packed my suitcase, said goodbye to my mother, boarded Mohawk Airlines, and traveled to Iowa City, Iowa, via Chicago. My adventure in the Midwest had begun.

Iowa and Fort Des Moines

Iowa was a stark reminder that I wasn't in Kansas anymore (or at least Buffalo): farmland as far as the eye could see, interspersed with small cities. Iowa City was a typical college town, a liberal oasis in a conservative state. I loved my classes and quickly settled into the life of a graduate student: days filled with classes and nights at the computer center, the library, or the design lab. I knew I needed to get my degree in the two years of the program as I couldn't afford to stay any longer. That was a lot of pressure and meant that I didn't have time to take advantage of the many cultural and recreational opportunities on campus. Football in Iowa was huge and so different from Buffalo, where the football program had been voted out of existence. I never went to a game.

In 1969, the Vietnam War was in full swing. War protests were everywhere, even in Iowa, where liberal islands like universities stood out in contrast to the rural countryside. While my studies were going well, the war was a constant presence. In December, the first lottery drawing since 1942 was held to determine the order in which people would be called for induction into the armed forces—the draft. The lottery focused on people born between January 1, 1944, and December 31, 1950. I was born in 1947.

When I was in undergraduate school, I had a college deferment, but that ended when I enrolled in graduate school. I never thought I was destined for military service after failing to be accepted into the U.S. Air Force ROTC program in Buffalo, but as December approached, the possibility loomed. My girlfriend, Pat Ulbright, who was a senior at the University of Buffalo, was very concerned, as was my mother. Out of 365 potential birthdays, where would mine, September 6, fall? It had been determined that anyone with a lottery number of 195 or below would be classified as available for military service.

The lottery drawing occurred on December 1, 1969. On

that date, every graduate student in my dorm (and probably everywhere in America) anxiously awaited the drawing. On my floor, we ordered pizza, and everyone gathered in the lounge so we could monitor the drawing. The first birthday drawn was September 14. Close, but no cigar! Then April 24, December 30, and February 14. I began to feel better and more relaxed. *What are the chances my number will be called?* October 18 and then—September 6, my birthday. The sixth number selected. *You have to be kidding me.* Within minutes, Pat called, near hysterics, followed closely by my mother. I was numb as the other students consoled me for being selected—until some of their birthdays started to be called. I had no idea what the next steps would be, but in January, I received a notice to report to Fort Des Moines, Iowa, for a preinduction medical examination. The gravity of the situation hit home.

One weekday, at three o'clock in the morning, I boarded a bus with the other unlucky candidates for a ride across Iowa to the army induction center. The bus left Iowa City and began the trip to the induction center at the U.S. Army Training Center at Fort Des Moines. Normally, it would have taken only a couple of hours to make the one-hundred-mile trip. But our bus stopped periodically along the way to pick up young people who were making the same trip. I was struck by the attitude of the boys we picked up in rural Iowa. How different they seemed to me from my fellow graduate students. Most of them put on a show of bravado once they got on the bus, loudly proclaiming how they were going to fight the Viet Cong and protect democracy, while the students from Iowa City sat in glum silence, dreading the coming hours. Later, I reflected on the fact that the war was largely and disproportionately fought by men and women from low-income, rural, and minority communities. On my bus, it seemed like there were two entirely different populations—university students and farmers—being rounded up for induction.

Our bus arrived at the fort after about four hours, and we

exited into a large hall. Fort Des Moines was established in 1901 as a training center. African American officers were trained there during World War I, and it was one of the first centers where women began training for military service. It seemed a dreary place, perhaps in keeping with its role as the first step for many going into the military. The hall where we entered was filled with uniformed soldiers and other personnel along with hundreds of prospective soldiers, who were arriving on buses from all over Iowa.

After a period of basic paperwork making sure we were the people the recruiters had on their list, we went into a classroom for some basic written tests. I don't remember the tests directly, but I was left with the impression that they did not disqualify many candidates. From there we went into another large room, where we were told to disrobe down to our underwear and line up behind a yellow line. The line led to various stations where different medical tests were undertaken: blood pressure testing, hearing and vision tests, a check for any deformities, height and weight measurements, and who knows what else. It was very cold, and since everyone was in their underwear and barefoot, the process was very uncomfortable and degrading. On the other hand, the military was not too concerned with what we thought about the induction process, so long as it was both thorough and speedy.

Finally, you got to see a doctor. This was where the fun really began, because you could present the doctor with any evidence or documentation you might have supporting your claim that you deserved a medical deferment—the last chance you had to convince the military that you were not worthy of being a soldier.

During the entire process of following the yellow lines, many potential inductees carried papers or even briefcases with them for presentation to the doctors when the time came. Since there was no privacy whatsoever, everyone could hear everyone else who wanted to make a case to the doctors that they qualified for the much-desired deferment. There were many types of medical conditions that seemingly healthy men claimed to have. I heard people claim to have punctured eardrums, poor eyesight, ulcers, urinary tract issues, and on and on. One candidate produced X-rays, claiming he had spine deformities. The doctor in charge looked at the X-rays and ordered him into the city of Des Moines (accompanied by military police) to have independent X-rays taken to confirm that the images he presented were actually of him. I never saw him again despite spending more than eight hours in the induction process.

My mother had gone to see Dr. Romano, who had treated me for more than twenty years for a severe case of the skin disease eczema, and secured a letter from him attesting to the fact that if I served in a jungle environment, the condition would get much worse. It also didn't hurt that the air force, three years earlier, had disqualified me from the ROTC program because of the same condition: atopic dermatitis. I also had that letter. I carried both letters, hoping that maybe they would keep me out of the army but allow me to serve in some other branch.

One of the examinations was for any foot deformities, particularly flat feet. Lo and behold, I was diagnosed with flat feet. The doctor told me that was good for a medical deferment, but I had to finish the entire testing process before it would be finalized. I now had two medical conditions that would disqualify me from military service. The guy standing in line behind me asked me in a whisper if he could use one of my doctor's letters. Desperate people contemplate desperate things.

We left Fort Des Moines at about three o'clock in the afternoon for the journey back to Iowa City. I was happy with how things turned out and couldn't wait to tell Pat and my mother. On the way back, the bus was somber as most of the guys had not received medical deferments and were expecting to be called up for service within a few weeks. I knew the war was going badly and a lot of casualties were being reported, and I wondered how many of the boys on the bus would eventually become statistics themselves. No one said anything as we stopped at each rural area or small-town location to let off a passenger we'd picked up many hours before. This same scenario was being played out throughout Iowa and throughout the country. While I was grateful that I got to finish my graduate education, I never forgot that bus trip and Fort Des Moines.

Tornado

I saw my first tornado looking out my dorm window, moving across the plains outside of Iowa City. I remember my roommate, who was also named Bob and was a law student from Mankato, Minnesota, being amused that I was seeing my first tornado. I was fascinated at the sight until I was informed by the resident hall adviser that I had to go to the basement until the storm passed. I saw several more tornados during my two years in Iowa, but none, fortunately, ever hit the city. At the time, I thought tornados were limited to the Midwest. However, after moving south, I learned that tornadoes also impacted southern states. Just a few years ago, a tornado tore through parts of New Orleans. Even hurricanes that affected the Gulf Coast and the Eastern Seaboard have spawned violent tornadoes in recent years. So is it better to live in an area where you worry all season long about a hurricane in the Gulf that you'll know may be coming your way two or three days in advance, or is it better to have virtually no warning of a tornado? Neither choice seems ideal.

Hoarding Cookies

My dorm was across the Iowa River from the main campus, so you had to cross a bridge to get to class. One January or February, the state was hit with a major blizzard that closed the campus (and all the food facilities) for several days. No food could be delivered to the dormitories because of the snow, ice, and extreme cold. You couldn't go outside, it was so bad, and soon all the snack machines were emptied. However, my mother had sent me a box of cookies, and my roommate and I were careful to eat them only with our dorm room door closed as students began roaming the floor looking for anyone who had some sort of food in their room. Even in the worst Buffalo weather, I didn't have to worry about running out of food!

The Baltimore Experience

Arriving

To get a master's degree in my city planning program, in addition to the regular classroom requirements, you had to write a master's thesis and participate in a summer internship at some type of city planning agency. Today, many students don't write a thesis. Some do what's called a major paper or a major project. But fifty years ago, it was required. It's the same with the requirement for an internship, which today is often waived—but back then, it was required. I went to Professor James Harris and asked for his help in finding a three-month internship in the summer of 1970, one that, hopefully, would also yield a thesis topic. Professor Harris contacted one of his former students, Joe Mertz, who worked in the city planning department in Baltimore and who arranged for a paid internship there—*paid* being the crucial term here, since I had barely enough money from my scholarship and loans to live in Iowa City, let alone another city. On May 1, I headed to Baltimore in my old Volkswagen.

I didn't realize it then, but Maryland was a border state during the Civil War and as such was essentially the middle ground between North and South. I began my journey south by stopping in Baltimore, arriving in the evening on a Thursday in the pouring rain—naturally. Professor Harris had arranged for me to stay with his former student for a couple of days while I looked for an apartment. Joe lived just on the outskirts of the Central Business District, on a street that ran from the CBD to the suburbs. Charles Street, for all practical purposes, divided the city into east and west Baltimore, and in the center of the city, it contained block after block of picturesque row houses. Many of those houses looked similar: brick front, three or four stories, steps leading up to the front door. In the pouring rain, it was hard to distinguish the buildings and even harder to see the addresses on them. Once I found the correct street, I got out of my car and went directly up to several buildings before I found the right address. I parked the car several blocks away on an adjacent street and knocked on the door.

No one answered, so I kept knocking for several minutes. *Great*, I thought. *Here I am for the first time in Baltimore, where I know no one, in the rain as night is falling and at the place where I'm supposed to be staying—and no one is home!* However, just as I was about to give up and was contemplating staying the night in my car, a man came to the door in his underwear.

After inquiring about who I was and remembering that I was the guy who was supposed to arrive that evening and spend a couple of days with him and his wife looking for an apartment, he told me to come back in an hour as he was "getting busy with his wife"! Then he shut the door. What to do? Nothing to do but go back to my car and wait.

When I went back, Joe let me in, introduced me to his wife, and set me up for the night. The next day, she and I went around looking at apartments, which luckily were plentiful, and within a few days, I had signed a temporary lease on a sparsely furnished apartment and moved in. After a rocky beginning, I was looking forward to starting work for the Baltimore City Planning Commission.

Parking the Car

The planning commission's offices were downtown, about a fifteen-minute drive from my apartment, but I hadn't yet gotten a transit map, so I asked my hosts where I should park my car as I was going to drive to work on my first day. There was plenty of parking available a few blocks from the office, they said, and although the area was a little iffy, that was where I would get the best rate at a parking meter. So early on Monday morning, I drove down to the recommended area, excited to begin my internship at a real planning office.

My hosts were right that the area was a little iffy. It was near the water in the Inner Harbor area with a lot of commercial and warehousing uses. I quickly found the parking area that they had recommended. It was almost under an overpass, and the parking meters were surrounded by trash, abandoned cars, and homeless individuals meandering around.

As I parked the car, I noticed one individual coming in my direction. A large man, he wore soiled pants and an old winter coat—which seemed odd, since it was May and much too warm for a coat. He needed a shave, a haircut, and treatment for skin sores. I rolled down my window and saw he was carrying what can only be described as a filthy rag.

"I'll wash your windshield for five dollars," he said.

Not being very familiar with what was clearly going down, I said, "No thanks, I'm good."

His stare said he knew he was dealing with either someone with a mental illness or just a plain idiot. "I don't think you understand," he said. Then I noticed that in his other hand, he held a brick. "This is not a very safe area, and sometimes car windows get broken when someone throws a brick through the windshield. A brick like the one I have in my hand. Or tires get slashed and cars get keyed. Now, for only five dollars, not only will I clean your windshield, but I will be sure no one throws a brick, like this one, through your window and slashes your tires or marks up your car."

Now, I was pretty naïve and slow on the uptake, but even I recognized the options that were being offered. My car was an old Volkswagen, but still, it was valuable to me, and after work I still had to walk back to this area to claim it. Suddenly, five dollars seemed like a good investment. I paid the man and then said it was not necessary to wash my windshield—as I was pretty sure if he put the rag on the glass, the window would dissolve. He took my money, said, "Good decision," and walked away. I got my car after work and never parked there again, choosing to walk or take transit rather than pay the going protection rate.

Fells Point

Pat and I were getting married at the end of the summer, so every dollar was precious. After a few weeks, I realized I needed to find a way to get out of paying rent for my small apartment. For my internship, I was placed by the assistant planning director, Bernard Berkowitz, in the neighborhood planning division of the Baltimore City Planning Department and was assigned to the Northwest Baltimore neighborhood area around the Pimlico racetrack. I became friends with the planner assigned to this area as I shadowed him to meetings and strategic planning sessions. He and another planner were renovating a townhouse in the Fells Point neighborhood, a rapidly gentrifying area bordering the Inner Harbor redevelopment area. The Inner Harbor of Baltimore was just beginning a transformation from a working maritime area to a glitzy entertainment and tourism district, which eventually contained the Baltimore Aquarium, the Maryland Science Center, and a complex of hotels, bars, restaurants, and music venues. But in 1970, that transformation was just beginning, and it was a hardscrabble area bordering downtown and the historic Fells Point neighborhood.

The planners understood that I was getting married and

needed to save as much money as possible. They said I could live in the townhouse for free as it would provide nighttime security for their ongoing renovation. Of course, I would sleep on a mattress on the floor, but the price was right, and I jumped at the chance. I vaguely knew that the neighborhood was working class and had a reputation for being somewhat dangerous, but I figured if I went to and from work in the daylight, it shouldn't be too bad. In addition, the Fells Point location made it possible for me to park my car next to the townhouse and walk to work. As a bonus, my work with the planners gave me access to lots of meetings and helped me develop a topic for my thesis, a technique of community engagement called a charette (a meeting or series of meetings in which stakeholders attempt to solve problems and conflicts in a rapid and focused manner).

About a block from the townhouse was a Pentecostal church, which had set up shop in a vacant commercial storefront. It had a large neon sign outside advertising the church and inviting all comers. I had to pass it coming and going from my new residence. The prayer service always contained music and, frequently, loud chanting and praying. One night, coming home (I came home after dark much more often than I originally intended), I noticed that the church was having a service, and I decided to stop and see what was going on. I entered and stood in the back. I expected that people would notice me and invite me to participate in the service, but that wasn't the case. Communicants were all singing and swaying to the music, hands extended toward the sky and, for many, eyes closed. There were many amens and "Thank you, Lord" pronouncements. There were people who appeared to be talking gibberish, whom I later learned were speaking in tongues. It was a hot summer night, and everyone was sweating profusely. If I remember correctly, someone had a snake they were handling in the front of the church.

Soon I became concerned that the prayer service seemed

to be getting out of hand as the yelling, singing, and chanting got louder and louder. I was gradually making my way to the door when someone grabbed my arm and tried to steer me to the front. Several other church members also wanted to help me get saved, and they pushed me toward the front. With considerable effort, I broke away, hurried out the door into the narrow street, and quickly made my way to my townhouse. Halfway down the street, I could still hear the music and chanting. On several occasions, when I passed that location, the church had people on the sidewalk and even in the street urging passers-by to come in and join the congregation. Often the police would be called because of the loud sounds coming from the storefront. I'd had enough of the type of religious fanaticism being practiced down the street, and I learned to take a more circuitous route when coming home at night.

Going South

"A journey of a thousand miles must begin with a single step."
—Lao Tzu

At the end of the summer of 1970, Pat and I got married and returned to Iowa for me to complete my graduate education and prepare to start my career. I received three job offers as graduation in the spring of 1971 neared. One was from Minneapolis, another from Leavenworth, Kansas, and a third from New Orleans. We had had enough of the cold weather in Buffalo and the Midwest, so New Orleans was an easy choice. We were going south.

The Trip

After I received the job offer from the New Orleans City Planning Commission, Pat and I packed up our Volkswagen, closed our bank account (taking out our last $100), and drove to my parents' house in Buffalo. We had so little money and were so anxious for me to begin my new job that I missed the graduation exercises so we could get started on the trip to New Orleans. I borrowed $400 from my mother, and Pat's friend Sharon Casper arranged for us to stay with an acquaintance in New Orleans until we could find an apartment. We said goodbye to our friends in Buffalo and began our trip south.

As we made our way south, it occurred to me that we were going to travel through cities that seemed to have little connection to the large rural areas we were passing through. New Orleans was a major international city and was known up north as an exotic locale for jazz, bourbon, and Mardi Gras as well as for its reputation as an "anything goes" town where you went for a good time. The states we were passing through, including Tennessee, Alabama, Mississippi, and then rural Louisiana, were completely foreign to us. We wondered: Why would anyone go to these states? In the years to come, many of my relatives moved from New York State to Florida, particularly the area around Orlando. We didn't consider Florida part of the south, just a vacation or retirement destination.

Frankly, traveling through southern states to reach New Orleans was a little frightening, since we always seemed to be hearing reports of attacks on northern college kids going south to participate in the Civil Rights Movement. We determined to make as few stops as possible and to stay on those portions of the interstate highway system that were open for as long as possible.

In 1971, the federal interstate highway system was not fully completed. On many of the routes, you would be driving on the divided highway and then have to exit and get on a local road, which usually ran parallel to the under-construction interstate segment, until you could resume your trip on a completed section. If you were unfamiliar with the area, you were totally dependent on signage to guide you on local roads.

After we crossed into Alabama, we were forced to exit Interstate 65 as we were coming into Birmingham and continue our trip on local roads. It was brutally hot, and our car did not have air-conditioning, so starting and stopping on local roads became very uncomfortable very quickly. We were traveling through a suburb of Birmingham when we came to an intersection where signage directed us to make a left turn to continue on the local road that, we hoped, would connect with I-65.

As I began my left turn from the left-hand lane, I noticed that the car in the right lane was attempting to make a left turn as well, even though all the signage made it clear that left turns were to be made only from the left lane—the lane I was in! As the driver made his turn and crossed in front of me, I couldn't swerve because I would have gone into the oncoming traffic lane, so I collided with him. We both stopped. Because our cars were going slowly, there was little damage. Pat and I were both very upset to be involved in a traffic accident with a New York State license plate in sweltering temperatures. We didn't have to wait long before a police cruiser arrived and a very tall, crisply dressed officer got out and came over to the accident scene. He asked the other driver what happened, and when the driver spoke, it was with an accent so severe I could not understand what he was saying. Then the officer turned to me. I was nervous but fairly confident that the other driver would get a ticket since he was making an illegal left turn when he turned into me. I was wrong. The officer told me I was at fault and would get the ticket. He said I could accept the ticket or contest it, at which point he would arrest me and take me to jail, where I would await a trial to plead my case. Very politely, I said I would accept the ticket. What choice did I have? We were young people in a strange city, driving what could be described as a hippy-looking Volkswagen from New York, and we had no money to stay in Birmingham to contest the ticket. "Yes sir, no sir" made up the bulk of my answers to the officer's questions. So despite the fact that the other driver was clearly at fault, I accepted the ticket, and we continued our way.

We finally left Alabama and entered Mississippi on a local road. As we made our way south, we passed through small town after small town. Confederate flags along with the state flag of Mississippi were flying on every gas station we passed. We were acutely aware that it had been only sixteen years since fourteen-year-old Emmett Till was lynched in Mississippi in 1955 and eight years since Medgar Evers was assassinated in

1963 in Jackson, Mississippi. I made certain to follow every speed limit to avoid being stopped by local police. Along those rural roads, we saw unbelievable poverty that went on mile after mile: ramshackle houses that were barely standing, African Americans sitting on porch steps or on the ground. We passed a man sitting on a plywood sheet that had four wheels, pushing himself forward on his hands—it was his only means of locomotion. It was absolutely shocking. Sure, Buffalo had areas that were poverty-stricken, but nothing like this. It could have been another world.

Finally, we pulled into New Orleans in the early afternoon, the temperature a reported ninety-six degrees. As we made our way down Veterans Highway toward the apartment where we'd be spending a couple of nights, I thought, This is the hottest I've ever been—and it's only June.

The Haunting

What good would a book of stories centered on the South be without a tale of a haunting? New Orleans has its share of supernatural stories—whether they're about the Baroness de Pontalba or the voodoo queen Marie Laveau—in which ghostly apparitions appear to inhabit homes, businesses, or even parks. Indeed, a tale close to home involves the ghost of Mona Lisa in City Park. Legend has it that Mona Lisa was the daughter of the wealthy family who lived in a mansion located on park grounds called the McFadden Mansion. In one telling, the daughter is said to have fallen in love with a sailor, whom her family disapproved of. She was so brokenhearted and distraught that she dove into a nearby park lagoon and drowned herself. The spirit of Mona Lisa is said to inhabit the grounds; numerous people have reported sightings of the specter, including sounds of yelling and strange laughter. In all my years in the park, I never saw her ghost, but who knows—maybe I wasn't in the park at the exact moment Mona Lisa made her appearance.

I have another haunting tale, this one set not on park grounds but close by. In April 2019, I was sitting in my office at City Park late on a Friday afternoon. Most of the other employees had already gone home for the weekend, and I was preparing to do the same when my phone rang. After the bitter controversies over the removal of Confederate monuments in the city, including in City Park (which I will relate in another story), I had generally stopped answering my phone unless the caller ID showed it was someone I knew. Better to let the call go to voicemail so I could answer the calls that were important and ignore those that angrily opposed the removal of the monuments.

But for some reason, I decided to answer this call. It was from an Alex Wilder, and the call was coming from California. Mr. Wilder explained that he and a partner, Eddie Dyer, had purchased a restaurant called Christian's not too far from the park in the Mid-City area of New Orleans. Christian's was in a historic Lutheran church, which was built on the property in 1914 and converted to a restaurant many years later, in 1977. Okay, I thought, what does this have to do with me? Mr. Wilder explained that they had been having difficulty developing a marketing strategy for the restaurant. They had called the local councilman to seek his advice and ask if he could recommend someone who could help them, and the councilman recommended that they call me. While I was flattered at being recommended, I couldn't fathom how I would be able to help them develop a marketing strategy for their restaurant. Mr. Wilder told me that while he was in Los Angeles, he had a feeling that something was pulling him to New Orleans, and so powerful was the feeling that he and Mr. Dyer bought the restaurant sight unseen.

Then Mr. Wilder said, "Oh yeah, and by the way, the restaurant is haunted to the max!"

After purchasing the building, Mr. Wilder and Mr. Dyer realized that it suffered from foundation issues, not only because of its age but also because it had flooded during Hurricane

Katrina. Structural engineers were brought in to stabilize the building; they later told the owners they did not know how the building was still standing since the entire foundation of the structure was near collapse. Mr. Wilder maintained that some mysterious force kept the building from collapse because it was its destiny to be saved.

The building was stabilized and renamed Vessel, and staff were hired. Soon after, the owners noticed that they seemed to be going through a very high number of employees. While high turnover is not necessarily unusual in the service industry, theirs was abnormally high, and they began to ask their team about why.

The culprit was the weird happenings that seemed to occur frequently at the restaurant. Waiters felt as though they were being pushed down the stairs by an unseen hand. A coldness would envelop the staircase inside the building even on very warm days. Drinks started flying off serving trays. Doors that were locked became unlocked. Burners on stoves suddenly ignited, and dishwashers and other equipment repeatedly broke down even though they were new. Managers in an upstairs office reported frequently feeling a light touch on their neck, and perhaps weirdest of all, a bright orb was seen floating and circulating in the back patio.

To help them understand what was going on, the owners sought the assistance of researchers from the television program The Dead Files, which investigates paranormal activities. The researchers brought in sophisticated equipment designed to detect the presence of spirits, searched the city's property records to unearth the history of the property, and even brought in Marielle Songy, a psychic who consults with the program.

It turns out that the land underneath the building had been owned by Micaela Leonarda Antonia Almonester y Rojas—the baroness of Pontalba. Born in 1795, the baroness, best known for construction of the Pontalba buildings flanking Jackson Square, had a troubled and sometimes violent marriage, which led to her being shot by her father-in-law. Some believe that the bright orb floating in the patio is actually the baroness reincarnated. Adding to the mystery were the findings of the psychic, who said she felt an angry presence in the building—including hearing the cries of those who died in a hospital nearby. The hospital, named after former U.S. Representative Lindy Boggs, was flooded during Katrina, and numerous patients died after being stranded with no power, food, or water for many days after the storm inundated the city.

Mr. Wilder asked that I visit the restaurant and let him know any thoughts I had about how to market the property. How could I not go! In May, I visited the restaurant with friends—Linda Landesberg, Evelyn Audler, and Steve King—had dinner and talked with several members of the staff. All said the same thing—"Haunted to the max!"—and they told us about the various types of hauntings they had experienced. Creepy, spooky, eerie was how they characterized their experiences. Several believed the baroness inhabited the building, and all reported seeing the floating orb firsthand. While we did not experience any of the hauntings, we were impressed that the staff had all experienced some type of unusual phenomenon.

I called Mr. Wilder and told him it was clear to me that the marketing of the restaurant should emphasize the characterization of the building as haunted. Don't hide from it, I told him. Embrace it! In a city and state that are full of tales of ghosts and spirits, the fact that the building appeared to be possessed in some manner could be a marketing plus.

The restaurant is still there at 3835 Iberville Street. Visit it—and let me know if you see the baroness!

The School Dilemma

In 1973, Pat became pregnant with our first child, and Jennifer Lynn was born in February 1974. Like all new parents, we faced choices about childcare, but we didn't worry much about regular school as it seemed so far in the future. But before we knew it, 1979 rolled around. We had moved into the Faubourg St. John neighborhood from Broadmoor, and the question of what school to send our little girl to was before us.

In New York State, the question of what elementary school to send your children to was never really a question because there was virtually no choice. You sent your child to the neighborhood public school: period, end of story. I attended PS No. 71, a few blocks from my house. Only those parents who were wealthy or who wanted a religious education for their children even contemplated private school. No one Pat and I knew in Buffalo or Johnson City (where Pat grew up) ever went to a private elementary school. It just wasn't done. In general, the public schools were top-flight educational institutions and prepared children well for high school and then college or vocational training.

In New Orleans, we found a very different situation. Many of the neighborhood public elementary schools were not graded very highly and were in old, rundown facilities. If you wanted your child to attend one of the few highly rated elementary schools and you did not live within the district that school served, you had to secure a permit from the school board. The other options were private schools, of which there were quite a few, and religious schools, of which there were also quite a few. Many private or parochial schools were in suburban areas where white families had been moving to avoid sending their children to an integrated school. Private or church schools were funded with tuition and fees, which often were thousands of dollars a year. That kind of money was out of the question for us, so since we lived out of district for the elementary school we wanted, we applied for a permit to send Jennifer to Hynes Elementary in the Lakeview section of the city.

We were fortunate in that the principal, Judee Morovich, was looking for parents with elementary school–age children. After we applied for the permit, we went to see Ms. Morovich, who was the poster child for what an elementary school principal should be. Strict but empathetic, Judee ran a tight ship and was interested in helping potential students get a permit—which we did, in August. Jennifer stayed at Hynes from kindergarten through sixth grade, which was where Hynes ended.

When we came to Hynes, like most parents, we wanted to be involved in the school, and Pat became a member of the PTA while I joined the Dads Club. This organization, promoted by the principal, was her way of ensuring there would be some level of male involvement in the school. After a couple years, I became president. Hynes Elementary, one of the finest public schools in the city, had no air-conditioning. In New York, school started after Labor Day, but as we soon discovered, in New Orleans, school started in August, one of the hottest months of the year. When we attended events or activities in the school, the heat seemed unbearable to me. It seemed comparable to schools having no heat in the winter in Buffalo. I resolved to find a way to install air-conditioning in Hynes. Of course, most dads and moms felt the same way, and for two years, we lobbied the school board relentlessly to include air-conditioning in its capital budget. It took time, but we finally had cool air when Jenny was in the fourth grade.

Eventually, all our children attended Hynes: Jenny, Kelly, and Ryan to the sixth grade and Amanda to the fourth grade. All received permits to attend except Ryan, as by the time he went to elementary school, we had moved to a house within the Hynes district. When your child reached the sixth grade in the New Orleans public school system, your choices of where to send them for middle school or seventh or eighth grade were limited. Again, in Buffalo, there was no choice. I went to PS No. 82, the public middle school, before I started high school at Kensington High School.

We decided to send Jenny to Eleanor McMain, a public school offering seventh and eighth grade in a location across town. It seemed to have a good reputation, and we knew virtually nothing about private schools as an alternative. It turned out not to be a good choice. Jenny was bullied on the school bus and in school. It was rough. We determined not to send any of our other children to a public middle school.

When our second child, Kelly, reached sixth grade, we began looking for an alternative to McMain. I had come to know Dr. Fritz Wagner through my position as an adjunct faculty member at the University of New Orleans College of Urban Planning. One day, while I was discussing the middle school dilemma with Fritz, he suggested we look at the Louise McGehee School, an all-girls private school located in New Orleans's Garden District. His wife, Margaret, was headmaster and was looking for girls to attend her school. At first, Pat and I thought there was no way we could afford the tuition at a prestigious girls' school. However, after meeting with Margaret and touring the school, we asked for a tuition proposal, and Kelly received a substantial tuition grant, which made it possible for her to attend. At the same time, Margaret wanted girls for the lower school and made another grant available to us for our youngest daughter, Amanda, to join the fourth-grade class. Amanda eventually attended McGehee through the eighth grade, while Kelly stayed through high school. Our youngest son, Ryan, attended through the sixth grade, and again, we were forced to consider a private school for his middle school years. He attended St. Paul's Episcopal School for seventh and eighth grade before going on to high school. Both Pat and I had become Episcopalian, having converted from the Lutheran Church (me) and the Catholic Church (Pat). Ryan became our only child to receive part of their K–12 education at a religiously affiliated school.

So our school dilemma was solved for elementary school by applying for and getting permits for the girls to attend an out-of-district school and moving within the district for our son. Then, after a forgettable experience for Jennifer in public middle school, we sought private education for middle school for Kelly, Amanda, and Ryan. There was only high school left.

The premier public high school in New Orleans was Benjamin Franklin High School, and it was located in the uptown area of the city before moving to a new site on the campus of the University of New Orleans. It was an outstanding school with strict entrance requirements. Kelly was happy and successful at McGehee, which went through high school, and Margaret wanted her to stay, so we opted for her to remain in private school. Jennifer, Amanda, and Ryan all wanted to go to the gifted public high school, so one by one, they applied to Franklin and were accepted. They all received an outstanding education and participated in various sports. All the kids went to college well prepared—Jennifer to University of Arkansas, Kelly to Texas Christian University, Amanda to Clemson, and Ryan to Princeton—and all went on to advanced degrees.

School choices in New Orleans were difficult as we moved from public to private to religious institutions. Some parents were able to afford a private or religious-oriented education for the entire K–12 experience, while others mixed and matched. It was so different from northern schools. Navigating the school dilemma in New Orleans was stressful and expensive. I think it remains so today.

My Third Most Embarrassing Moment

In 1973, Mayor Landrieu, the planning commission, and the business community, represented by the Central Area Committee of the New Orleans Chamber of Commerce, determined that it was necessary to revise the plan for the Central Business District. After much consideration, the partners hired the internationally known city planning firm of Wallace, McHarg, Roberts and Todd (WMRT) out of Philadelphia. The firm, founded by Harvard classmates David Wallace and Ian McHarg in 1963, had produced groundbreaking plans for the Inner Harbor of Baltimore and the Plan for the Valleys in Maryland, among many ecological and CBD plans for both American and foreign cities. Dave Wallace and Ian McHarg were arguably two of the most influential and widely known architects and planners of the early 1970s—real rock stars of the profession.

Harold Katner and I represented the planning commission in the study. What an opportunity for someone who had been with the planning commission for only a couple of years! Regular meetings with the mayor and his staff and the most prominent members of the business community usually did not involve so junior a staff member as myself, but I appreciated the faith Mr. Katner showed in me, and I jumped right into the process.

After hiring WMRT, a few members of the partnership flew to Philadelphia to meet Dave Wallace, who was the partner in charge for the firm, and his team to discuss the approach to the study and how we would engage members of the community in the effort. Wallace invited the group out to dinner at one of Philadelphia's finest restaurants. To me, this was the equivalent of having dinner with Buckminster Fuller, I.M. Pei, or any of the planning and architectural superstars of the era.

In the restaurant, I sat next to Wallace. I was beyond excited. Menus were passed around, and when the waiter came to take our orders, Wallace ordered first. He chose steak tartare. For those of you not familiar with the dish, it consists of raw ground beef, usually served with onions and mushrooms. The operative word here is raw! When my turn came, I was so nervous sitting next to the great man that I ordered steak tartare as well, not knowing that it involved raw meat. I thought steak tartare was like a filet mignon or a rib eye—or maybe it was a type of Philly cheesesteak.

When the main dishes arrived, I was appalled at the slab of raw meat on my plate. Dave Wallace immediately dug in. He was thoroughly enjoying his dish. I, on the other hand, was frozen. I tried to eat the vegetables served on the plate. However, soon I could no longer hide not having tried the raw meat. I was totally embarrassed and desperate not to be revealed as an ignoramus who clearly should not be in the company of the distinguished planner, let alone other members of our party who had flown all the way from New Orleans to kick off a major effort of the Landrieu administration.

Do you remember various episodes when the Three Stooges, faced with a similar dilemma—being served inedible food at a fine dinner table—looked to get rid of it by hiding it under the table or dumping it in a flowerpot? Those were the thoughts that raced through my brain as other diners were finishing their main course but I hadn't started mine. So, channeling my best Moe Howard, I tried a variety of similar tactics. First, I deliberately dropped my fork on the ground, and when I bent over to retrieve it, a small bit of steak tartare went with me to be deposited under the table. Gross, but desperate men do desperate things! Then I leaned way back in my chair and deposited some more material in a large planter bed behind me. Finally, when I thought people were somewhat distracted, I moved my cloth napkin subtly over the remaining meat and picked it up, hiding it in the napkin. Panic-stricken, I couldn't look at Wallace, hoping he didn't see any of my efforts. If he did notice, he never said a word, nor did anyone else at the table. How no one saw any of my hidden food tricks, I will never know. But the dinner ended with everyone toasting a successful study and me trying to hide my red face.

Lagniappe: Once when I was in a meeting with Darryl Berger, a prominent real estate developer, about an important riverfront project, he kept saying that "Big Mo" was on his side. I wondered who Mo was, certain he was not in the room. Later, one of my staff confided in me that Mo was short for momentum! The developer thought he had big momentum on his side to complete the project. Who knew?

The Cult

Everyone believes that no matter what park they happen to be in, it's "their" park. They're often oblivious to others using the same park, and many of them have absolutely no record of having helped the park in any manner. Nevertheless, it's their park, and they have the right to do anything they want in the green spaces.

One day during Halloween week, I got a call from someone who claimed they represented a religious organization that wanted to have a Halloween service in Audubon Park. Now, we often had small groups of people from a variety of religious affiliations carry out services of some sort, usually composed of guitar playing and singing or prayer services or simply watching the sun rise. Most of the time, they did not even inform park management of their activity because it was so small and nonintrusive. Having someone call about a service was unusual.

The person informed me that they represented a satanic organization, they would have about twenty people present, and their service would mainly consist of chanting various incantations. Being very aware that parks are traditionally open to a wide variety of free speech functions, protest activities, and even religious services, I initially didn't see any reason why their request to hold religious services shouldn't be approved. So I described the normal conditions we attached to those kinds of events: no amplified music, no interfering with other park visitors' enjoyment by aggressive proselytizing, no cooking or food preparation, and, of course, no weapons of any sort. I also suggested, as I often did, that they employ a police officer to be sure they were not bothered by other park guests. The caller said these conditions would pose no problem. Then he said, "During our services, we create a circle that we set fire to and then chant around the flames."

Say what?

"We perform our services right at sunset, so it's very dramatic when we set fire to the ground."

I was momentarily stunned but recovered in time to say, "You cannot set the park on fire!" And before he could add anything to his description of the religious service, I said, "And absolutely no animal sacrifices or anything involving live or dead animals."

After a brief silence, the caller said it would not be a traditional Halloween service without the fire, whereupon I suggested that he take his service elsewhere because under no circumstances were we going to set fire to the park. Which he did.

The Denver Blizzard

During the time the Audubon Nature Institute was developing its off-site breeding facility in the 1990s on the west bank of the Mississippi River, I was tasked to be the liaison between Audubon and the U.S. Fish and Wildlife Service. The USFWS is the federal agency charged with enforcing the Endangered Species Act and protecting and promoting the wildlife of the United States. It also approves breeding programs involving endangered species, and since the main purpose of the off-site facility was to breed animals that were endangered in the wild, it was important for Audubon to have a strong relationship with the federal agency. Audubon also had a relationship with the National Park Service (NPS) and its Denver Service Center, where almost all NPS capital projects are designed.

The USFWS office that oversaw endangered species permitting and construction activities was also in Denver—more specifically, in the suburb of Golden, Colorado. As part of the relationship, its personnel visited Audubon and the breeding facility, and I made frequent trips to Denver to brief the USFWS on the progress of constructing the center. If you've ever flown into Denver, you know that even on the best of days, the airport is a windy destination and not for the faint of heart. I didn't like flying into Denver in the summer, let alone in the winter, but that is what I found myself doing one January.

I was scheduled for a three o'clock flight out of New Orleans, but the departure time kept being moved back because of bad weather in Denver. (That should have told me something right there.) I had had lunch in a Mediterranean restaurant that did not agree with me, so I was not feeling the trip from the get-go. As the delay got longer, I became more agitated.

Sometime around ten o'clock at night, the plane departed from Louis Armstrong International Airport for the roughly three-hour flight to Denver. Then we began to encounter turbulence, which turned more severe the closer we came to Denver. The plane was barely occupied, so everyone had an entire row to themselves, which was good, since most of us were trying to hide how concerned we had become. Nevertheless, around one thirty in the morning, the plane landed in what, as I peered out the window, appeared to be a blinding snowstorm.

As we exited the plane, most of the passengers seemed to have to have no luggage to claim, and they left the airport immediately, grateful to be on the ground. I had checked my luggage, so I headed for the claim area and was surprised to find that I was the only passenger waiting for my bags to appear. I waited for a long time until my bags finally came tumbling down the conveyer belt. It must have been two or two thirty in the morning by the time I picked them up. There was no one around: no one in the baggage claim area, no one in the information booth, and most importantly, no one in the rental car area. This was a serious problem as I'd been expecting to rent a car to drive to my hotel and, eventually, on my business with USFWS.

Uncertain what to do, I grabbed my bags and proceeded to exit the airport terminal, where I confirmed what I had seen from the plane: there was a violent blizzard underway. The wind was howling and the snow coming down so fast and so strong that I could barely make out the areas beyond the terminal. Clearly, being outside in the snow and cold with nowhere to go was a bad idea. I decided I would go back into the terminal and attempt to contact the hotel to see if they could send a car or a van to get me. I reached for the door and found it had locked behind me. I went from door to door and found they were all locked and there was not a soul to be seen. The thought struck me that maybe I would freeze to death outside the terminal at Stapleton Airport!

I took my bags and began walking down the concourse. My prospects looked grim. Then, at the far end of the concourse, I saw the Delta flight crew coming out of the terminal and getting into a van that was obviously there to pick them up. I began running (as best I could through the snow, on a slippery surface) toward the van, yelling at the top of my voice for them to wait for me. For a moment, I saw the van begin to pull away, and I felt my last hope vanishing before my eyes. Then it stopped, and the driver got out, looked at me, and finally motioned for me to come over to the van and get in. I'd never been so grateful to get into a warm vehicle. I had no idea where the van was even going, but I didn't care. It had to be better than being locked outside the Denver terminal at two o'clock in the morning in a blizzard.

I thanked the flight crew and the driver for waiting for me, and off we went to their hotel. The van driver then drove me to my hotel, a service above and beyond what I could have expected. I never again went to Denver in the winter!

A Son of the South

The history of both the North and the South is intimately tied to the Civil War, something that I never fully understood while living and going to school in Buffalo. Although there are many numbers thrown around, it is generally believed that between six hundred thousand and eight hundred thousand soldiers perished, with an undetermined number of civilian casualties. Even now, over 160 years after the end of the war, feelings still run high on both sides of the struggle.

In July 2015, Mayor Mitch Landrieu appeared before the New Orleans City Council to request that the legal process for removing four postwar monuments dedicated to heroes of the Confederacy begin. The four monuments were statues of Confederate generals Robert E. Lee and P.G.T. Beauregard; the president of the Confederacy, Jefferson Davis; and a memorial to the Battle of Liberty Place at the foot of Canal Street. These monuments were erected after the war in an effort driven by what was often characterized as the Cult of the Lost Cause.

Because the South lost, many in the South searched for a justification for the war and a substitute for victory. Many Southerners attempted to create an image of the war as a heroic epic, a clash of two civilizations: one the North and its way of life and the other the South, with its much different way of life. This representation attempted to portray the South as waging a noble and heroic struggle against a powerful enemy intent on destroying Southern culture and institutions. One ubiquitous form of expressing the beliefs of the Lost Cause was the erection of public monuments throughout the states that had seceded from the Union. Sometimes the monuments were justified as public art or as memorials to veterans.

Of course, Northerners saw the conflict differently. In their view, the war was an illegal rebellion to preserve slavery, and the leaders of the Confederacy committed treason against the United States.

Many of the monuments erected in support of the Lost Cause theory were in public parks and open spaces. (Many streets in Southern cities were also named after Confederate generals; after the removal of the four monuments, New Orleans began a process to rename those streets.) The public space at the entrance to City Park contained a statute of General Pierre Gustave Toutant-Beauregard. P.G.T. Beauregard, who was born on a plantation in St. Bernard Parish, just south of New Orleans, resigned his commission in the U.S. Army to join the Confederate army in 1861. He will forever be remembered as the Confederate officer who started the Civil War by ordering the firing on Fort Sumter in April 1861.

After years of fundraising by the Beauregard Monument Association, the statute of General Beauregard was completed and erected in 1915 in an elaborate public ceremony on land made available by City Park. It had stood at the entrance to the park for one hundred years with little attention paid to its symbolism until Mayor Landrieu and leaders in the African American community pointed out that the statute, along with the other Confederate monuments, was a symbol of hate, bigotry, and intimidation.

In December 2015, the city council, after months of debate, declared all the monuments public nuisances and ordered them removed. It took the city more than a year to marshal the resources to remove the statutes because of the threats of violence against the private contractors who were going to do the actual work of taking them down. During this period, various people argued that City Park should exercise its rights as "owner" of the statue to prevent its removal.

Lawsuits were filed to prevent the removal, and protests in various forms focused on the park, its board, and its staff. Periodically, protestors would show up at park board meetings or hold signs and walk up and down in front of the park's administrative offices. Members of the park's staff, if they were wearing their uniforms, were harassed at restaurants or confronted in stores and businesses by supporters of the statue. Even after the statue was removed, stones painted with the names of Confederate leaders were thrown into the circle where Beauregard's statue was located, along with a voodoo doll adorned with pins. Members of the City Park board also faced harassment from friends and acquaintances who supported one side or the other of the debate. They received phone calls, emails, and visits to their homes as they tried to balance friendship and upholding the authority of the park. More than one hundred years after the Civil War ended, tensions were high.

As the chief executive officer of the park, I often felt the weight of the controversy and was continually bombarded with visits, calls, and emails from citizens on both sides. Many of the phone calls were so vile that I stopped taking calls if I could not identify the number and let them go to my voicemail. Finally, the city moved in 2017 to remove the statue using a contractor whose personnel were masked to protect their identity and guarded by many city police. The statue was taken to a location in east New Orleans, and a warehouse was erected around it to protect it from vandalism and from those who wanted to retrieve it and place it in another location in Louisiana.

One day, after the statue had been removed, my phone rang. The call was from an unknown number. For some reason and against my better judgment, I decided to take the call. Almost immediately, the caller started shouting at me. He demanded to know if I was the one responsible for letting the city take the statue. (Like I could have prevented its removal!) He continued to berate me, saying I had allowed a sacred piece of the South's history to be removed and should resign immediately. Finally, in desperation, he summoned his last bit of anger and yelled, "You should be embarrassed to call yourself a son of the South!"

For a moment, I was unsure how to respond. Finally, I explained that I was not born or raised in the South, could not be a son of the South, and was never going to be a native Southerner! With that, he hung up.

Foreign Adventures

"Adventure is worthwhile in itself." —Amelia Earhart

Although I have not traveled overseas much (my daughter Kelly has visited over sixty countries), those places I have seen have been pretty exotic. I've been to Kenya and Tanzania in Africa and Indonesia and New Guinea in Southeast Asia. The following stories are of those adventures.

Africa

Periodically, the zoo (also known as Audubon Nature Institute) offered its members the chance to go on a safari to photograph animals in their natural environment. Most of the trips went to Africa as it offers the best opportunities to see the greatest variety of exotic animals. These trips were often led by members of the administrative staff accompanied by key members of the animal staff, who could provide commentary and explanations about the animals and their behaviors. These trips were wildly popular with not only the members but also the staff who accompanied them. It was considered a real perk if you were selected to go.

In July 1994, I was asked to lead a group of zoo members to Africa. Roger Isles, who was the curator of mammals, was chosen from the animal staff to accompany us since most of the animals we were likely to encounter were mammals, such as lions, leopards, buffalo, rhinos, and a great variety of hoofstock. My job could basically be described as herding cats: making sure everyone had their required vaccinations, knew when to show up at the airport, and kept the number of bags they were bringing under the limit; constantly reminding the group to pack their passports and visas; sending lists of appropriate clothing; and making a point of having guests bring more than one camera and lots of film (remember, this was the 1990s, before the widespread use of digital cameras).

Our group consisted of thirty-one people in total, and in August 1994, we flew to Africa. We traveled from New Orleans to New York, where we met Joyce Baisal of Fun Safaris Tour Company at the South African ticket counter and then boarded a fourteen-hour flight to Johannesburg. After staying overnight in a Holiday Inn, we flew to Nairobi, Kenya, where we were to begin our safari. The return trip would consist of flying back to Johannesburg and then back to New York and on to New Orleans.

Landing at the Nairobi airport was a stark reminder that we were not in Kansas anymore. Soldiers in full military gear armed with automatic weapons were everywhere. We were warned by the tour company not to allow any of our tour group to take pictures in the airport, something Roger and I had to reinforce on landing.

In Nairobi, we stayed at the New Lord Stanley Hotel and had dinner at a restaurant on the outskirts of the city called Carnivores, which specialized in serving wild game. We dined on zebra, giraffe, wildebeest, and crocodile and then returned to the hotel. The next morning, we left to begin our adventure.

During the roughly two weeks we were in the bush, we visited the Maasai Mara, a massive national park, and stayed at the Sweetwaters Tented Camp and the Aberdare National Park in Kenya. Our main tour guide gave us basic instructions on appropriate protocols as we began our trip.

Everyone was required to sign up with the Flying Doctors

Society of Africa. The flying doctors were necessary as we were advised that if anyone was hurt or injured on the safari, we would not be sent to any hospital in Kenya or Tanzania as they were considered unsanitary and inadequately staffed. You paid a special fee to be flown out of the country to a hospital considered adequate by the society. In addition, we were advised never to put on our shoes or boots in the morning without shaking them out in case something had crawled into them during the night. Both men and women were advised never to shave with a straight razor, which might cause you to bleed, because the risk of infection from any open wound was so great, and never drink any liquid that did not come from a sealed bottle that you saw being unsealed in front you. Finally, everyone must take their malaria pills religiously. Yes, we were not in Kansas anymore!

On the Maasai Mara, we saw zebras, wildebeests, warthogs, giraffes, lions, hyenas, Thomson's gazelle, impala, oryx, and eland. In the Aberdare National Park, we stayed at the ARC, a hotel that overlooked a small lake and a salt lick that attracted many different types of animals at night, including elephants, rhinos, and Cape buffalo.

Of course, during the trip, one of our group lost their camera and had to borrow an extra camera from someone else in the group. Once, when seated beside a river, guests ventured too close to a barrier that prevented Nile crocodiles from coming out of the river and had to be cautioned to get back. On another occasion, we came across a bull elephant. How big, you might ask? Think National Geographic big! We stopped the van to give the elephant a wide berth, and a woman on our vehicle who was having trouble getting a good photo asked me if I could step outside the van with her camera and get a good shot. I'm sorry, did you say get out of the van with a bull elephant who's flapping his ears and raising his trunk less than fifty yards from us to take a picture? Now, I am no animal expert, but I was pretty sure we'd warned our party to never get out of a safari vehicle no matter what the circumstances! I politely said I couldn't do that, and after a short wait, with plenty of opportunity to take pictures, the elephant went on his way.

Special options were offered if safari-goers wanted to pay extra to experience them, such as flying to Lake Victoria to go fishing or taking an early morning balloon ride over the Mara. Kitum Cave, which is a short distance from Lake Victoria and is sometimes visited by people going to the lake, is often cited as the possible origin of the deadly Ebola and Marburg viruses, because the cave is inhabited by bats that can carry the diseases. Fortunately, no one from our party chose to go to the cave. I chose the balloon ride, which was truly spectacular and ended with a champagne breakfast on the Mara, surrounded by armed guards in case the local occupants of the park—lions, hyenas, and so forth—decided to join in.

One afternoon, we went to a Masai village. The village huts were surrounded by a circular wall of thornbushes to protect the villagers from roaming lions. Because the Masai raise cattle, the animals were brought into the village at night to protect them from the lions as well. The result was not something Westerners were used to since the cattle relieved themselves in the village during the night. The Masai were skilled traders, and we traded with and bought a variety of goods from them. Roger and I even managed to buy authentic Masai spears, which was a highlight of the visit. (Back then, we never gave a thought to what issues bringing them on the plane might cause.) The spears were at least six feet in length, and our guide told us that these were the spears the warriors carried on their game hunts. We were also told that the Masai believe a young man becomes an adult when he kills a lion with his spear—an extreme act of courage.

One day, we visited the Aberdare Country Club, which was a retreat built by the British in the colonial heyday of their occupancy of Kenya. British army officers and bureaucrats would come to the country club for R&R. It was truly a relic from the past but beautifully maintained. It contained a restaurant, a gift shop, a hotel, a swimming pool, and even a par 66 golf course. The rules of play reflected the unique location of the course. Rule no. 2

stated: "'Relief of 6' will be granted if the ball lies on animal hoof marks on the green." Even more to the point, rule no. 8 stated, "Relief given should ball be taken by a baboon—free drop given."

On our final night in the bush, the group had a farewell dinner, and we gave out various awards to members of our group to recognize their contribution to our adventure. Some of those awards included:

The Best Pickup Line Award—"I just flew in from Nairobi!"

The Butt Award: For taking the most photographs of animal butts while on safari.

The Sharing, Caring, Sensitive Guy of the '90s Award: For being the man who refuses to go down with his bus when baboons fall from the sky. (One day, a baboon jumped on top of one of our vans while we were cruising, and we all thought Roger should shoo him off—something Roger didn't agree with!)

Mark and Richard Engstrom received an award for losing or damaging the most items on safari. Marbury Little received an award for being the person most likely to get into a fight while on safari. One of our merry band received an award for consuming the most alcoholic beverages on the trip. I received an Honorary Audubon Curator Certificate award.

The next day, we got on a plane in Nairobi for the return trip. As we boarded the plane, the South African stewards sprayed disinfectant directly on our clothes as a precaution against transporting the tsetse fly, which can carry trypanosomiasis, or sleeping sickness, from sub-Sahara Africa back to South Africa—once again proving we were not in Kansas anymore.

A final thrill occurred on the flight back to New York as the plane had to make a stop for fuel, which it did by landing in complete darkness in the middle of the ocean. Everyone was grateful when the plane was able to take off after taking on fuel and we could proceed home.

A few weeks later, the zoo hosted a photo party where everyone brought copies of their favorite photos of animals to share. It was truly a trip to remember.

New Guinea

Background

The following stories about New Guinea need a bit of background, which comes from a variety of books and articles and from my PhD dissertation.

During the time I worked for the Audubon Nature Institute, I was also an adjunct professor at the University of New Orleans in the College of Urban and Public Affairs. I taught a variety of courses to both graduate and undergrade students, including an introduction to urban planning, recreation planning, and even a course in real estate development.

The dean of the college, Fritz Wagner, and two other professors in the Planning Department, John Wildgen and Jane Brooks, had developed a friendship with a PhD student, Joseph Molyneaux, who was director of corporate security for PT Freeport Indonesia. Freeport, which began as a company mining sulfur in southern Louisiana, had in 1966 received exclusive rights from the Indonesian government to explore and mine minerals in a large area of the Indonesian province of Western New Guinea. After discovering significant new ore deposits, over the course of several years, Freeport expanded its operations such that by the early 1990s, the company's rights encompassed over twenty-four thousand acres, and its workforce had grown from an original one thousand workers to nearly ten thousand.

Freeport had built a variety of capital facilities to support its mining operations, from port facilities in the lowlands on the Arafura Sea to upgraded power plants and worker housing in a town called Tembagapura further toward its mine in the highlands. However, the tremendous expansion of mining operations prompted Freeport to consider the need to maintain an effective, productive workforce in one of the most inhospitable and remote regions in the world. In order to address the increased need for additional living areas, recreational facilities, guest accommodations, administration buildings,

and expanded logistical and support facilities as well as ground and air transportation systems, Freeport determined that it needed to construct an entirely new town in the lowland region. Joe Molyneaux felt that Freeport needed help in devising government structures for the new town as well as consulting on housing and community engagement. Wagner, Wildgen, Brooks, and I were engaged to provide that support. In October 1994, the UNO team traveled to New Guinea.

A word about New Guinea. The Republic of Indonesia controls the western portion of the island of New Guinea and considers it one of its provinces. The capital of Indonesia is Jakarta, and it lies at the extreme western end of the world's longest archipelago, comprising over 13,000 islands and stretching some 3,400 miles. Western New Guinea lies at the eastern end of the island chain, and thus there is a huge distance between the government center to the west and the province to the east. You reach Papua New Guinea either by flying through Australia or flying from Jakarta and island-hopping. A trip from the United States usually includes nearly forty hours of sustained travel.

The term remote doesn't begin to describe the conditions and the people of the island. The entire island is covered in a dense tropical forest, with extensive mangrove swamps located at sea level, rain and cloud forest in the interior, and steep mountains covered in the world's only equatorial glacier at the center of the island, where Freeport's mine is found. In the place where Freeport operates, extreme variation of geography and climate occurs within a short stretch of fifty to seventy miles: from the mangrove swamps on the Arafura Sea to the snowcapped top of the Puncak Jaya mountain peak. Annual rainfall of between one hundred and two hundred inches makes the forest virtually impenetrable and serves to isolate the Indigenous peoples and tribes of the area.

While Indonesians are generally described as being of Malay origin, related culturally and linguistically to the populations of the Philippines and the Malay Peninsula, the Papuans (the name given to the various tribes of New Guinea) are more closely related to Australian Aboriginal peoples. Until relatively recently, the Papuans were extraordinarily isolated not only from the world but also from each other because of the difficulty of the terrain, the impassability of the jungle, and the steep and rugged mountains, resulting in hundreds of small villages that had little if any contact with each other. Of the world's six thousand known languages, one thousand exist only in New Guinea as isolated tribes each developed their own language—unintelligible to one another.

Often described as primitive, the peoples of coastal New Guinea were often thought to still practice headhunting—and indeed, in 1961, Michael Rockefeller, the son of New York State Governor Nelson Rockefeller, vanished along the coast of southwest New Guinea and is widely believed to have been killed and eaten by members of the Asmat tribe.

Indonesians (in my opinion) generally look upon the Papuans as inferior and not of the same intelligence as the peoples of the rest of the island nation. Thus, there is a constant tension between the government and the population it controls, with independence movements constantly advocating for New Guinea to break away from Indonesia and establish its own government. This is actively resisted by the Indonesian government because of the rich natural resources of the island, including a variety of minerals, timber, and fisheries. For many years, Indonesia has stationed troops on the island to protect the companies harvesting these resources and to put down independence movements. Freeport has initiated a wide variety of programs to help the Indigenous Papuans adjust to the modern world, including employing them as miners and security personnel while developing diverse agricultural products and even some basic manufacturing. The Papuans have also embraced a nascent tourist industry where they market their native carvings.

This is the environment in which Freeport sought to build its new community; our group of academics and practicing urban planners hoped to help.

1994

Our group first visited New Guinea in 1994 and made a repeat visit in 1996; I traveled there by myself in 2000. On our first visit, we flew from New Orleans to Los Angeles and then on to Sydney, Australia, and from there to Cairns, on Australia's northeastern coast. The final leg was a flight in a company plane from Cairns to New Guinea and the village of Timika, located in the lowlands not far from the sea. Joe thought it would be important to see the mine and all the supporting facilities, including meeting expat executives stationed on the island, before traveling to Jakarta to meet government officials and Freeport's environmental, real estate, and social programs staff.

Despite the fact that we were exhausted from the long flights, we immediately began our initial tour of the facilities. We received a briefing from a variety of Freeport officials on the challenges Freeport was facing with the mine expansion and in building the new community in the lowlands. These challenges included the difficulty in building and selling housing to Indigenous peoples who had no concept of land ownership, how to develop training and education programs for the Papuans, the difficulty of relating to workers from Jakarta versus the Papuans given the great disparities in education and sophistication between the two populations, how to treat expat housing in the new community—and most importantly to us, how to set up a government that would run the new town and be representative of the various tribes in the mine area as well as the Western employees of Freeport.

We visited the village of Timika, which one day would become much more populated as people from other parts of Indonesia traveled to the area seeking employment. Initially, the new town would be open to Freeport employees only. We also visited a business incubator, an art center to preserve and promote Indigenous cultures, and a school, all sponsored by Freeport. We then visited the maritime facilities on the sea.

At the end of our tour, we went to the Sheraton Hotel, which was built by Freeport and operated by the Sheraton chain. As there were no other modern lodging facilities in the entire area, construction of the hotel was necessary to house government dignitaries traveling to the mine and the great variety of Western employees who came and went. We finally had dinner and collapsed.

To make the point of how isolated this part of the world is and how hostile the environment: The next morning, I went on a short stroll outside the hotel (defying instructions not to) and proceeded to go right up to the edge of the rainforest where the landscaping of the hotel stopped. I then took one large step into the forest, and as I did so, it closed around me such that when I looked back in the direction I had just come from, I could see nothing but forest. I knew that if I took two or three more steps, I would be completely lost and unable to return to the hotel grounds. As Dr. Wagner once remarked, using a line from the movie Predator, "If you get lost here, you are in a world of trouble!" So I took a step backward and fell out of the forest into the grassy area surrounding the hotel. Lesson learned.

The next day, we traveled by helicopter to the Grasberg

mine. The mine itself, located high in the center of the island at an altitude of more than fourteen thousand feet, was an awe-inspiring site—it felt like the top of the world. Huge trucks, steam shovels, and graders constantly stripped away soil to harvest the ore, in which was embedded copper and gold. Only about 1 to 3 percent of the dirt harvested contained copper and gold, so it took a tremendous amount of strip mining to extract the amount of minerals necessary to make the entire operation profitable. The ore taken from the mine had to be transported more than one hundred miles and over fourteen thousand feet—from the top of the mountain through the cloud forest and the tropical rainforest—down to the sea so it could be loaded onto boats, which took it to smelters in Spain and other countries. It was impossible to move the ore in trucks through the dense forest terrain, and therefore, another method had to be employed. That involved creating a slurry by infusing the ore with water and sending the slurry down pipelines to the coast. Once by the sea, the water was separated from the soil, and the ore was loaded onto boats.

The cost of mining and extracting the copper and gold from staggering amounts of soil and transporting it from the top of the world to the bottom was huge. Added to these costs were the large sums required to build support facilities, such as the company town of Tembagapura. Considering that everything necessary for the mine to operate—from tires to nails to shovels, clothing, trucks, Jeeps, radios, helicopters, pipe, and so on—had to be shipped to the island, it was an economic necessity for a constant cash flow from the sale of the minerals to be maintained. This necessitated the uninterrupted flow of ore from the mine to the smelters and then to world markets.

Everywhere along this long chain of activities was the possibility that unforeseen events would cause the flow of ore to stop. Mine equipment might break; labor unrest could cause a slowing or stoppage of excavations; fuel, necessary to run equipment and power generators, might be delayed in reaching its destination; the pipeline carrying the slurry through the forest might break or be sabotaged; or key personnel might become sick and need to be transported to Australia. Any one of a thousand different scenarios could occur.

However, the president and cofounder of Freeport, James Robert "Jim Bob" Moffett, a Texas oilman, would accept no excuses for interruptions in the delivery of the ore. Countless times, we heard Freeport personnel exclaim, "The boats must be loaded every day!" Each day, a freighter was expected to pull up to the port facilities on the Arafura Sea, and each day, the expectation was that the ore, having just been dewatered, would be loaded onto the boat for the long trip to the smelters. If no ore reached the smelters, no copper could be sold and no revenue received. It was impressed on us that the success of the new town was to be another link in the chain that would help ensure success of the mine. No pressure here! Reflecting the fact that Freeport was pretty much the entire economic engine for central New Guinea and thus was able to demand any resource it needed to keep the mine producing, employees also were frequently heard to say, "If you own a hammer, the whole world is a nail."

During our stay, we met with a variety of Freeport officials, including Bruce Marsh, the environmental manager, to discuss environmental issues in the new townsite (at full build-out, the new town was to encompass over seventeen thousand acres, including forest preserves and national parks); Gaylord Watkins, the principal lawyer, to discuss options for new town governance; Dave Francisco, the general manager of Tembagapura; and Ron Landry, a vice president of communications, to discuss the difficulty of getting people from the rest of Indonesia to move to New Guinea considering that Javans considered the Papuans almost savages.

After finishing our tour, we flew to Jakarta for more meetings with senior Freeport officials and lengthy discussions on what would be considered the success of the new town, what was Freeport's relationship with the Indigenous Papuans, and what did the company want from the new town. Other topics included what would happen if Indonesians in Jakarta refused to move to New Guinea, what would be the relationship between the new community and the existing village people, and what type of government structure would be acceptable to Indonesia. Finally, we met with Paul Murphy, a Freeport executive vice president, to discuss Mr. Moffett's vision for the new town, including it becoming a regional center and providing a better quality of life for expats, Papuans, and Indonesians.

We followed up on our trip with a visit to Jakarta's port and zoo before flying back to New Orleans, where we continued our discussions over the next year and a half and crafted a report outlining some recommendations on options for new town government structures, phases of new town growth, and ways Freeport could improve relations with the Indigenous tribal people.

1996

Professor Jane Brooks, Dean Fritz Wagner, and I returned to Indonesia in January 1996 for a second trip—once again, a very long journey. From New Orleans we flew to Los Angeles and then on to Tokyo and then to Singapore, where we took a quick tour before our flight to Jakarta and then to Timika in New Guinea.

The flight from Jakarta to New Guinea was aboard an Indonesian carrier, Garuda Airlines. The plane was packed with mine workers going to the Freeport mine for their tour of duty. I believe the three of us were the only Westerners on the flight and probably the only ones who did not speak Indonesian. The flight was a long one, necessitating a stop at Penang International Airport on the island of Sulawesi (also known as the Celebes), which is about halfway between Java, where Jakarta is located, and Timika, in New Guinea. Sulawesi is the eleventh largest island in the world and consists of remote regions, a mountainous hinterland, and a great diversity of flora and fauna. And it's wet! The island receives rain almost daily and absorbs over 460 inches in a year.

As we approached the airport, the pilot announced that the landing could be rough. (At least that's what we thought he was saying when we noticed all the miners putting on their seat belts.) It was a bright, sunny morning above the cloud layer that suddenly became much darker as we descended through the clouds. It was raining, and the plane was buffeted by high winds when we broke through; we could make out the tops of palm trees swaying in the wind. The plane was descending, and soon we could make out the contours of the ground—but no runway. There was concern on many of the miners' faces, but since we had never flown into this small airport, we assumed there was plenty of runway for us to land on. Bad assumption! As the pilots judged we were going to miss the runway, the plane's engine roared, and we started a steep climb—back up through the clouds and rain into the bright sunshine. The plane banked, and soon we realized the pilots were going to try again. We came back down through the clouds at a steep angle as the crew was determined not to miss the runway again. Bobbing and weaving, we descended through the deluge until the ground came up suddenly and we hit the runway hard, the plane braking on its slick surface. We finally rolled to a stop, turned, and went back to the small airport. I unstuck my hands from their grip on the armrest.

I think this is another of the experiences that has led to my fear of flying. More on this later.

After refueling, we resumed our flight and landed in Timika on Saturday, February 3. We were taken to the Sheraton, where Fritz and I went to the bar and discovered it was Mexican night, with a Filipino band playing Mexican songs and country music tunes. The bar was full of Australians and South Africans, all associated with Freeport. What a weird situation!

We resumed our meetings the following day and had lunch with David Lowry, who was the force behind many of the social programs Freeport was attempting to launch. David, an Episcopal minister from New Orleans, especially wanted to emphasize how the Indigenous peoples of the island could benefit from the new community. We also learned that the community was to be named Kuala Kencana (KK).

Later that day, we met with Richard Browne, an executive vice president of PT Alatief Freeport Infrastructure Corporation; Dr. Marvin Clark, an expert in malaria control; Charlie White, who supervised Freeport's efforts at sustainable development; and others who were responsible for working with the native Papuans. These meetings further confirmed the difficulty in building a new Western-style community in one of the most remote places on the planet.

On Monday, we visited Kuala Kencana, various aspects of which were under construction, including the first phase of worker housing. The center of the new town included office buildings, a large, grassy central area where sports could be played, and two religious buildings, one a church for Christian employees and one a mosque for Muslim employees. While KK was going to be Freeport's base of operations for the entire mine project, everyone agreed that Timika must become the center of the region. But how to accomplish this goal when Timika was growing organically and KK was a completely planned community with tight building and aesthetic controls? It was such a strange situation: a modern community with utilities, recreation spaces, power stations, religious institutions, and wide roadways becoming a reality while the supposed center of the region had none of these improvements. We got down to discussing the minutia of running a small modern city, including debates on subjects such as whether there should be a fee to use the recreation spaces and what would be the affirmative action programs Freeport would sponsor to train Papuans for jobs and teach them how to live in modern houses. (During my visits to residential areas, I routinely saw women cooking in pots outside the houses they were assigned, despite the fact that each house had a modern kitchen.) We discussed how security could handle squatters who set up camps just outside KK, how education programs would be established, and whether there would be an internal system of transportation. We spent the rest of the week in meetings and writing a draft report of our recommendations. In many ways, we sympathized with the Freeport staff and their difficulty in understanding how the new town would implement Mr. Moffett's vision for both the community and the mine.

We made time for some sightseeing and souvenir hunting at small shops staffed by native artisans. We hoped to take a trip to see the remote Asmat tribe but were told that tensions were too high at the present time. We left Timika and again stopped in Sulawesi before arriving back in Jakarta.

On the trip home, we decided to fly to Europe and visit a medieval city in Belgium on the North Sea, historic Bruges. From Jakarta, we boarded a plane for Singapore, which then flew to Paris, where we connected to another flight to Brussels and then a train to Bruges.

On the flight from Jakarta to Singapore, I happened to notice that, on the television over our seats, the flight could be tracked so you knew where the plane was at any given moment. About halfway across the South China Sea, I saw the image of our plane, and it was superimposed over a swirling mass beneath us. I asked Dr. Wagner what that mass was, and he calmly informed me that it was a typhoon. We were flying over a typhoon! Another disturbing flying experience.

We managed to make a brief stop in Singapore and then went on to Paris and Brussels. We stayed the night in Brussels and took overnight bags for the train ride to Bruges. A beautiful and historic medieval town on the North Sea, Bruges is a huge tourist destination—but not in February! It was brutally cold, and few restaurants or museums were open. We toured the town, bought chocolate (something Bruges is famous for), stayed several nights, and then took the train back to Brussels to catch a flight home.

Once back in New Orleans, we drafted working papers and a final document outlining our recommendations so far and a suggested course of action for the company. While our team stayed in touch with Freeport for most of 1996, the company determined that we had fulfilled our contract and that it was not necessary for our team to return to New Guinea. It was an amazing experience and one that few university professors and practicing planners will ever have. I, however, was not through with New Guinea.

2000

David Lowry was aware that I was a PhD student at the University of New Orleans and that I intended to use the development of Kuala Kencana as the subject of my dissertation. He also knew that I had not finished collecting the data necessary to write my dissertation after the trips in 1994 and 1996, and he offered me the opportunity to return to KK to finish my research. I, of course, jumped at the chance and made a return visit to New Guinea by myself.

On this trip, I stayed not in the hotel but with David in expat housing on the grounds of the new town. I did not have transportation from the hotel to the town, so this made it much easier to visit parts of the new town on foot. Over the course of several weeks, I walked all the residential areas that had been constructed, doing a census on the number of housing units and the population within each unit. In 2000, there were approximately 1,800 residents in the new town, composed of Papuan workers and Westerners living in approximately six hundred housing units. The area around KK, especially Timika, had exploded, with many small businesses and an estimated population of seventy-five thousand. I finished my research and returned to complete my Doctor of Philosophy degree.

As I think back on my three trips to New Guinea, I am grateful to have had the opportunity to see one of the most unique places in the world. It is useful to note that the extreme isolation of the Papuan people—both in terms of the culture of the Western world and the extreme isolation they face in the rainforests and mountainous terrain—has exposed them to modern society in only the last one hundred years. Just as in other places in the world traditional societies are being transformed by their introduction to modern technology, cultures, and economic systems, so too are the Papuans trying to preserve their way of life while adapting to a new world.

This adaptation is made more difficult by the fact that the Papuans are governed by Indonesians who consider them inferior in every way to Indonesian society. Additionally, there is an American company that is trying to operate a mining business and, at the same time, has been tasked—by the government's lack of interest—with providing services and resources that would normally be the obligation of that government. Despite efforts by Freeport to assist the Papuans in benefiting from the mine, the Indonesian government has positioned the Papuan people so that they will never receive the benefits that are rightfully theirs as the ancestral owners of the minerals beneath their land. If they are a colony of Indonesia, they will live in the shadow of Jakarta. Were it not for the exploitation of the island's vast natural resources, it is doubtful that the government of Indonesia would have any interest at all in the Papuan people or their culture.

In what is unarguably one of the most remote locations on earth, a mountain is being systematically degraded, at least one boat is being loaded with ore every day, and a primitive people are struggling to preserve their heritage and a way of life that is vanishing. It is an unbelievable clash of cultures, and my experience of it is one I will never forget.

Lagniappe: After many long years of observing New Orleanians driving and utilizing public facilities, I have reached the conclusion that for our residents, signs are just suggestions. (Some readers in other locales may have come to the same conclusion.) Come to a full stop at a stop sign? No. Signal when changing lanes? Not necessary; it's just a suggestion. Obey the speed limit—any speed limit? No, that's for the other guys. Yield to oncoming traffic? Heavens no, not necessary—just a suggestion. Don't park in a handicap zone unless you are handicapped? No. This disregard is not limited to traffic signs. Put your dog on a leash? No way. Pick up after your dog? Yuck. Mandatory evacuations? Not me, I'm staying. Yup, signs are just suggestions!

City Park and Hurricane Katrina

"Start where you are, use what you have, do what you can."
—Arthur Ashe

In August 2005, just as we were beginning to make progress raising public funds and had just completed a new master plan for City Park, Hurricane Katrina laid waste to the city and the park. More than 80 percent of the park was flooded with four to eight feet of water, and every building was extensively damaged or destroyed. All our equipment was lost, and I was forced to lay off 90 percent of the staff as all our self-generating revenue sources were gone. This is the background to the stories that follow.

The Birthday Party

When my team and I returned from being evacuated, in early September 2005, we set up a makeshift office in a trailer that George Parker, our chief administrative officer, had procured from the state. One day in November, April Laughlin, who was pulling double duty as a salesperson for our catering operation (talking to brides who had their wedding receptions canceled) and as a receptionist at our trailer, told me that there was a woman at the front of the trailer who wanted to pay for a birthday party for her little girl. A birthday party? April tried to explain to her that all our facilities were damaged and we had no venue for such an event. But the woman began to cry, so April came to the back of the trailer to get me.

The woman tearfully told me that her house had been flooded and gutted. She could not have a birthday party for her little girl in a gutted house—and I had to help her. It was one of many heart-wrenching stories we heard of people who used to use the park for special occasions only to find it in ruins. I told her we would fix up something. Rob DeViney, our chief operating officer, who had virtually no staff for support, managed to get a pressure washer and clean off the Peristyle, a turn-of-the-twentieth-century bandstand where the park used to hold dances and other events. The staff also found some tables and chairs, and that little girl had her birthday party in the park. Tears all around.

Collecting Rent

In the months following the storm, it seemed like City Park had reverted to the days of the Wild West. Hundreds of contractors were camping in the park: there were no hotels or campgrounds open, so they sought the next best thing, which was putting up their tents and trailers and RVs in the city's central open space. They had descended on New Orleans to take part in the lucrative work of removing debris and cleaning up the city. Some were individuals drawn to the city for the work; others worked for some of the big contractors hired by the U.S. Army Corps of Engineers and other government agencies.

There was no power in the park and no form of communication: that is, no Internet, cell phone, or land line phone service and no fax machines. At night, all one could see were campfires and lights from the various contractors. Some enterprising individuals set up rudimentary stores in the Marconi Avenue neutral ground bordering the park to supply the campers with necessities. Some nights there was music run on battery power, and it was rumored that you could purchase almost anything in the encampments. I sent our few female employees home before it turned dark since there was no police presence to provide security.

The storm had destroyed all our sources of self-generated revenue, such as golf and driving range fees; shelter, sports field, and stadium rentals; concessions and amusement park funds; and money from the catering of events like weddings and parties. As our resources were few, I was forced to lay off most of the staff, and we were very worried that we would run out of what little money we did have. We needed revenue desperately, so I thought we should try to collect rent from the campers in the park. After all, they could be paying rent to hotels and other lodgings; why shouldn't they pay rent for the privilege of camping in City Park?

The staff thought I was crazy. How are we going to collect rent from all the campers spread out through the park? How will we keep track of the money? Do we offer receipts? If someone refuses to pay, how will we enforce payment? There were a hundred reasons why it would be impossible to collect payment from the contractors. But we had no money, and the contractors were making money from the city's misery, so I resolved to try.

I sent one of our remaining staff members out to the tent compounds to ask for payment and see how it would go. Soon he came back and suggested I send our lone City Park policeman with him as some of the campers were not receptive to paying anything and some were not sure we were even park employees. I did, and they went from tent to tent and RV to RV asking for $300 in monthly rent to remain in the park. We provided written invoices and receipts. Almost everyone we were able to contact agreed to pay once they understood that the funds were going to help the park. By late November, we had actually hired a company, Storm Force, to collect the rent and establish rules for the campgrounds, including daily cleanup and trash removal as well as payment timelines. Storm

Force even began charging for equipment storage, and for a time, they brought in portable showers and laundry service.

I estimate that at one time, we had over five hundred trailers, tents, and RVs in the park, and by the end of 2005, we had collected over $50,000 in rent. These were desperate times, and our City Park "pop-up campgrounds" were one of those desperate measures we had to take.

Necessity Is the Mother of Invention

Hurricane Katrina not only physically devastated the park but also wiped out all our sources of revenue, effectively rendering us bankrupt. We needed money in the worst way, and our success with the campers prompted us to look for other way to raise cash.

Our golf driving range was one of only a few driving ranges in the region and was a cash cow before the storm; now, it lay in ruins. The building that supported the range by selling the balls, golf gloves, and hats had taken on eight feet of water. Most of the mats from which the balls were hit had floated away, as had the baskets that held the practice range balls. The machine that picked up the golf balls from the range had been underwater as well and was inoperable. To complicate matters further, Kemper Sports Management, the company that operated the golf driving range under contract with the park, had left with no thought of returning to help us. Yet we felt that many golfers would like for the range to reopen as, in the fall of 2005, there were virtually no recreation facilities open in the entire metro area. We had strung a rope across one of our damaged tennis courts, and many people were coming out for a turn on what was, at best, a marginal tennis facility, so we knew how desperate people were for a sports outlet. But how were we going to get the golf driving range open amid the disaster?

Rob DeViney, our chief operating officer; Mike Marini, our

maintenance director; and I went to the driving range and developed a plan to get our cash cow up and operating.

First, we had to collect golf balls. You can't have a facility where people pay to hit golf balls without the golf balls. Most of the balls were out on the driving range since none of them had been picked up when the mandatory evacuation order was given just a couple days before the hurricane hit. There were some balls left in the damaged building, but most were out in the field. How do we pick them up? Old-fashioned manual labor. We worked with our remaining staff to walk the range and pick balls out of the dirt and mud. Then we went in search of our mats and baskets, which had floated all over the northern part of the park and even across Bayou St. John, which ran alongside the range. The clubhouse had no electricity, and mold had already begun to set in from the floodwaters. But in an amazing contradiction, the building, after being ruined by water, still had running water, which we used to clean the mud off the balls we had collected.

We had a tent, which we brought out to the driving range, and we put the golf balls we had collected into the buckets we had salvaged. Normally, you could purchase a small bucket of balls or a large bucket. However, since we had no ability to make change, we decided to charge ten dollars a bucket whether the bucket contained many balls or a smaller number. We salvaged a table and two chairs, made a handwritten sign saying the range was open and the price for a bucket of balls was ten dollars, put the sign on the tent, and sat down to see if any customers were interested in hitting balls amid all the destruction.

Literally within minutes, cars began pulling up with people asking if the range was open. When we confirmed it was, they asked if we had any golf clubs. We didn't have electricity, let alone golf clubs, but we did have golf balls, and people told us they would go back to get golf clubs from their homes or wherever they were staying and bring their own clubs to the range. People started showing up and hitting golf balls, and we began collecting ten dollars a pop.

We congratulated each other on being brilliant managers who had taken a ruined golf driving range and turned it into a moneymaking operation. However, we spoke too soon, and before long, we realized that we were running out of balls with no mechanical means of picking them up. More people were coming, and our supply of baskets with golf balls was running low. In desperation, we ran out into the range, while people were still hitting balls, and asked them to stop. We explained that we had no way to pick up the balls they had just hit and that for others to enjoy the opportunity they had experienced, we needed them to stop, walk out onto the range, and pick up balls. We did not know what to expect. Pick up your own balls so others could hit? Yet with hardly any complaint, they walked out and began picking up the balls.

We carried out this makeshift operation until our maintenance director could get the ball-retrieving machine operating and we had secured a trailer that took the place of our damaged building. By February 2006, the range had its power restored, and we had reopened permanently.

Even today, I am amazed at the ingenuity of our staff and the goodwill of our community in helping us generate sorely needed revenue. It allowed many to experience some degree of normality in very abnormal times. Necessity truly is the mother of invention.

Native Americans Set Up Camp

In November 2005, just two months after the disastrous impact of Katrina, our lone security officer, Chief Billy Bayle, came to me and said that a group of Apache Indians had come to the park and set up an encampment on Scout Island, teepees and all. Apparently, they had arrived the previous evening in the middle of a rainstorm. They'd been recruited by a contractor cleaning up debris in the city to provide labor and told they would have housing and be paid a good wage. However, when they arrived, the contractor was nowhere to be found, and somehow, they found their way to City Park.

We told them we had no facilities to support any type of camping operation and urged them to seek assistance from some nonprofit agency, but they said they were staying. Other contractors had begun illegally camping on park grounds: there were no hotels or any other type of accommodations open, so they brought their trailers and tents and set up shop. Various entrepreneurs also started selling food and other supplies to the new residents. In many ways, it was out of control, and since we had no means to evict anyone and the city's police force was busy elsewhere, the Native Americans just stayed.

After a few weeks, representatives of the American Civil Liberties Union visited us and said they were representing the tribe and we had to provide decent sanitary facilities, electricity, showers, and even recreation amenities for them. We politely explained that we had no showers or working bathrooms for anyone, especially people who were occupying the park illegally. They threatened to sue us, to which we responded, "Fine, go ahead."

The standoff continued for about two weeks, until one day we went to Scout Island to check on things and discovered they were gone. We believe that a medicine man from their tribe had arrived from Arizona and persuaded them to leave. Thus the brief occupation of City Park by Native Americans ended.

Urban Wildlife

In almost thirty years of managing large urban parks, my team and I experienced many interactions with urban wildlife. Here are a few of our most interesting encounters.

In 2019, our park police received a call from a woman who claimed she was the victim of a vicious goose attack. It appears the lady was walking behind the Timken Center (the building that now houses Café du Monde in City Park) when she observed one of the park's wild fowl (a Canadian goose) calmly walking toward her. According to the police report, the lady stated that "without any warning or provocation, the goose ran to her and began pecking away at her left knee." She ran from the goose, which kept following her until she outdistanced him and reached a safe place. She received bruises to her left knee and told our officer that she expected us to remove the vicious goose from the park. We never had another report of a goose attack.

For whatever reason, our amusement park is an attraction for a wide variety of critters. We have removed numerous beehives from the area, including ones purportedly containing African bees. Racoons are a constant problem as they are attracted to areas that contain food and despite numerous warnings, guests feed them—which, of course, keeps them coming back. Racoons have large teeth and are very formidable animals when provoked despite their cute demeanor. Following Hurricane Katrina, City Park was overrun with many other kinds of animals, including snakes, rats, opossums, raccoons, feral hogs, and nutria, that water rat native to South America.

Canadian geese have taken up residence in area golf courses and are very prolific, making the playing of golf difficult.

Alligators are an ubiquitous presence in south Louisiana as well as being found in many southern urban parks that have large bodies of water. When gators are under four feet in length, the Louisiana Department of Wildlife and Fisheries will not pay to have a licensed alligator trapper remove them from a park. This, of course, just puts off the inevitable because small alligators get big and become a hazard to park visitors. How do alligators get into isolated park lakes and lagoons? We've caught people dumping small alligators into our lagoons because the animals they purchased as small reptiles for display in a terrarium outgrew the enclosure and are not manageable in a home. People seem surprised when their small gator, which Johnny thought was so cute, grows to three or four feet and threatens the family dog or cat. That's when they come out to the park in the dead of night and release the animal. Sometimes gators will walk into parks from a nearby body of water. When they do grow to more than four feet, parks try to contract with licensed alligator hunters to catch and remove them. This is often difficult: Alligator catching is something of a rare art as prices for alligator skins have not kept up with inflation and there is an absence of young people wanting to go into the profession. Who knew?

Coyotes have become an ever-present predator in urban parks as urban communities have encroached on their habitat, forcing them to enter urban areas to find food. Following Katrina, large groups of coyotes set up dens in City Park as we did not have the equipment or personnel to cut the grass to reduce the attractiveness of the park and there were no trappers available. Soon the situation was getting out of control: people were walking their dogs and coming into confrontations with packs of coyotes. It was a dangerous situation in 2006.

I happened to mention this fact to the police SWAT team commander, and he thought it would be an excellent opportunity to give his team some additional firearms training while helping us eliminate the coyotes from the park. Since coyotes are nocturnal hunters, he offered to have his team come out to the park at night to hunt the animals, which also worked for us since the park was closed at night and few people were out and about only a few months after Katrina. He arranged for his team to set up in an abandoned portion of the park with night vision goggles and sniper rifles.

Proving the old adage that the best-laid plans of mice and men often go awry, the commander came to see me about a week after his men set up in the park. He told me he would have to discontinue the operation.

"Why?" I asked. "Were you unable to find any coyotes?"

On the contrary, he said, his team found many coyotes. Unfortunately, there were a lot of other inhabitants of the park after dark besides the coyotes. Apparently, even though there were no lighted trails or areas where the grass was cut, large numbers of people were coming into the park at night to enjoy the reclusiveness it provided and conduct all manner of activities. In fact, there were so many people "using the park in the dark" that the SWAT team was afraid to get off a rifle shot once they spotted a coyote in their night vision goggles as they feared they would accidently shoot someone.

Even today, coyotes continue to occupy the park off and on when management practices have provided them with an environment conducive to their needs.

Odds and Ends

"The older I get, the more clearly I remember things that never happened." —Mark Twain

The following are stories that don't easily fit into a particular category or group. Some are medical stories (we all have those, right?), others are about flying experiences, and a few are about banking with ATMs. But they all happened, and I hope you find them interesting.

The Stress Test

During a routine annual physical when I was in my mid-sixties, my doctor suggested that it was time for a stress test to be sure my heart and arteries were in good shape. After all, he said, New Orleans, with its abundance of fried foods and spicy dishes, is the epicenter of unhealthy eating. Fine, let's schedule one, I replied. He told me I had a choice of two types of tests. In one, I would get on a treadmill and gradually work up to running as fast as I could; when I felt I'd had enough, I would stop, and they would take a reading. In the second test, I would be given a chemical that would speed up my heartbeat. I would run only a little on the treadmill before I could stop, and again, they would take a reading. After the test, I would rest for ten minutes before going home, and I could drive myself, so no need to inconvenience anyone else. After thinking for a minute, I decided to take the chemical test as I had a surgically repaired knee and didn't think I could run very fast on the treadmill.

On the day of the test, I arrived at a large medical office building run by my primary hospital, which housed many different specialties, including the cardiovascular department on the fifth floor. I went to the office, introduced myself, and completed preliminary paperwork that absolved the receptionists, the doctors, the medical assistants, the hospital, the testing laboratory, the owners of the building, the janitors, the lawn care company, and maybe even the mayor and city council from any liability whatsoever that might result from something going wrong with the test. Then I sat down and waited.

Soon I was ushered into a small office where they took my temperature, blood pressure, and weight. Then the medical technologist who was administering the test (doctors don't do testing anymore—it's beneath them) asked me if I had a history of heart disease in the family, scurvy, or Ebola before confirming that I had asked for the chemical as opposed to the stand-alone treadmill test.

We went next door to a room that had a treadmill and several chairs. I put on a hospital gown and had various sensors taped to my chest. Then the tech administered the chemical. I got on the treadmill and walked very slowly. For a few minutes, all was right with the world. I started feeling my heart beating as the chemical took hold, and it continued to build up speed. I began to get uncomfortable with the strenuous level my heart was working at, and I told that to the tech and her assistant in the room. They told me to get off the treadmill, which I did, but it had no effect on the rapid pace of my heart. I felt like my heart was going to burst through my chest. I sat down on one of the office chairs while the tech and assistant busied themselves with I don't know what. My heart beat on with, it seemed to me, increasing intensity. I was becoming very uncomfortable and thought I was experiencing what it must be like to have a heart attack. The medical team asked me how I was doing, and I said my heart wouldn't stop beating rapidly and I felt very much overwhelmed. The tech said, "What you need is a Coke." Apparently, having a Coca-Cola would counteract the chemical I was given.

"Great," I said, barely able to speak. "Give me a Coke."

"We don't have any on this floor," the tech said. "You'll have to go down a couple of floors where there's a soft drink dispensing machine you can use to get a Coke." I couldn't believe it. The problem was on the fifth floor, and the antidote to the chemical I was given was several floors below! I was still in a hospital gown and felt like I was having a heart attack, and I had to go down several floors to get a soft drink.

I told the team I needed to get a Coke in the worst way, but no one offered to go get me one or accompany me. So I dashed out of the room, through the waiting room, to the elevator bank—in my gown. I pressed the down button, holding onto my chest as if I could prevent my heart from bursting out of my chest wall. Finally, the elevator arrived, and I got on with other people doing their best to pretend they were not looking at the agitated man in a hospital gown and bare feet.

Finally, after what seemed an eternity, the elevator arrived at the right floor, and I virtually fell out, frantically looking for the soft drink machine, which I found in a small alcove a few feet from the elevator bank. I went to the machine, where I realized what you were probably already thinking: Where is his money if he's in a gown? I had no money, and the relief I was seeking was behind a glass wall for want of two dollars. As I looked wild-eyed around the room, a nurse of some sort came over to me and asked if I needed help. She reached in her pocket, realized she had no change, and said, "Wait here, I'll get change."

I leaned against the soft drink machine and tried to hold my heart in my body. Fortunately, the nurse came back quickly, retrieved a Coke, and gave it to me. I swallowed it, and almost immediately my heart began to slow down, color returned to my face, and my breathing subsided. I couldn't have thanked her more profusely.

After sitting down for a few minutes, I took the elevator back to the fifth floor and got dressed. On my way out, the tech asked me how the test went. I told them it was the last time I ever would opt for a chemical test. They seemed bewildered!

The Family Jewels

A few years ago, I was having difficulty walking and playing golf, so I went to see the orthopedic surgeon who had replaced one of my knees about ten years before, Dr. Derek Jones, who was chief of orthopedics at Ochsner Hospital. After an examination, he said I could have a torn bursa sac, and I was sent to physical therapy for several months to strengthen muscles around the sac. It helped but didn't alleviate the problem. I went back to the doctor, and he suggested a steroid shot might address the issue. Okay, sounds like a plan. Then he told me to take my pants off and get into a gown. Now very curious, I inquired where the steroid shot was going to be given. "In the groin," he responded.

Hold on! He was going to give me a steroid shot near the family jewels!

"Don't worry, we'll numb the area so you won't feel a thing," he said. Now, we've all heard that statement before from doctors, dentists, dermatologists. It is a prelude to various types of injections, and invariably, after hearing it, I've experienced some kind of pain, so the thought of an injection in my groin gave me pause.

But the doctor and his attending nurse insisted it would be no problem, would give me relief from the pain I was experiencing, and could solve the problem permanently. So

I got into the gown and lay down on the examination table, where I contemplated the ceiling for several minutes until I heard the door to the examination room open and saw the nurse wheel in a large machine with wires and computer keyboard, a screen, and a boatload of sensors. Somewhat alarmed, I thought it might be some sort of defibrillator meant to restart my heart should it fail during the injection. No, the nurse said reassuringly, this is just a monitor so we can follow the path of the needle into your groin and not accidently put it someplace it shouldn't go. Put the needle someplace in my groin it shouldn't go! Okay, because I'm a big believer in not putting needles into my groin where they shouldn't go.

The nurse placed the sensors all around my private parts, attached them to the machine, and tested them. Then she left. In a few minutes, both she and the doctor came back with a tray holding the needle and the steroid bottle. It was the biggest freaking needle I have ever seen. You can't be serious about putting this sharp object into my groin. Oblivious to my concerns, the doctor began to apply a numbing solution to the affected area. "Be generous with the numbing solution," I suggested. Then we waited a few minutes for the area to get numb, or at least as numb as it was going to be. I kept thinking, Why did I agree to this? Isn't this something that should be done under general anesthesia in a hospital?

The nurse asked if I wanted to see the needle penetrate and watch on the screen as the doctor manipulated the needle to insert it accurately right where he wanted it. I didn't even want to be in the room, let alone observe this long needle wandering around in my groin, so I declined. Alternately trying to remember who won the baseball Triple Crown in 1956 (Mickey Mantle) and wondering if I would be able to drive home after the procedure, not daring to think what would happen if something went wrong, I passed the next few minutes in a state of terror. Of course, there was some pain; I knew there would be. I felt the warm rush of the steroid being injected and then the relief when the needle was withdrawn. "All according to plan," the doctor said. "Just lie there for a few minutes before getting dressed, and the nurse will schedule you for a follow-up visit in three weeks." Then, as he was getting ready to leave, he said, "It may be necessary to schedule you for another shot in the same general area if you're not experiencing some relief to your pain."

After this adventure, I was sure that even if I was experiencing some pain, I was not going to tell him about it, because I was through having long needles inserted anywhere near the family jewels.

Lagniappe: Have you noticed that unless it is required by law, politicians at every level have stopped having press conferences? Or town hall meetings? Or public hearings? Or appearing in any format where someone might have access to an open mike or able to ask a question to which the reply cannot be pre-rehearsed? When is the last time your congressman, senator, or state representative held a press conference where members of the press or citizens could ask questions? Is it just because crazies grab the mike, or is it that politicos are afraid of making a mistake with an answer that will cost them the next election?

Thirteen Doctors

Not all medical stories are funny. In fact, most stories that revolve around illness or serious medical ailments have no humor about them. This is one of those stories.

In early August 2023, just a few months before my first book was published, I had my annual physical with my general practitioner, Dr. Matthew McQueen, and told him that I had begun to feel swelling in my hands and was having trouble gripping my golf clubs. (Now you know this story isn't funny!)

He recommended that I see a doctor who specializes in hand problems, Dr. Carol Meyer, a member of the extensive team of specialists at Ochsner Hospital. It took almost a month to get an appointment, but after X-rays, Dr. Meyer said that while my condition was not Dupuytren contracture, it was a swelling that might be alleviated by a steroid injection. Oh, and by the way, you have mild carpal tunnel syndrome in both your hands. The steroid shots were immediately helpful, so I didn't think much more about it.

Also in August, it was time for my yearly trip to the urologist to see Melissa Voltz, who, after a physical examination (we all know what that is), told me my prostrate was enlarged and ordered an MRI. By the middle of September, I had seen three doctors and Dr. McQueen's nurse practitioner.

As late September and early October rolled around, the swelling in my hands had come back and progressed to many other parts of my body. My knees, hips, neck, and shoulders all felt like they were experiencing some form of extreme arthritis or rheumatism. I had widespread aching, and all my muscles were stiffening. I had trouble standing, raising my arms, getting out of bed, and gripping a pen or pencil. It was truly all pain, all over, all the time. I had to buy special shoes because it was too painful to tie my sneaker shoelaces. I contemplated growing a beard so I wouldn't have to lift a razor to my face. My wife had to build up chairs with pillows as I could not lift myself out of our chairs or sofa. No one could help me because taking ahold of me caused such pain.

At the same time, I got to see a colorectal physician, Dr. Forest Johnson—my fourth doctor—who reviewed the previous month's MRI. He did not think there was anything immediate to be done and expected that Voltz would order another MRI next summer.

During part of 2023, I had also been experiencing shoulder soreness, so in October, after a several-month wait, I went to see Dr. Deryk Jones, head of sports medicine at Ochsner, who had already replaced one of my knees and my hip. After X-rays of my shoulder were taken, Dr. Jones told me he did not think shoulder surgery was necessary (thank God!) and prescribed physical therapy to treat the soreness. So, in November, I began physical therapy, even though I was in extreme pain from the aching in my joints. This was my fifth doctor so far, plus physical therapist Beau Moore at Innovation Science Center! In early November, I went back to see Dr. Meyer as my conditioned had worsened.

I felt that I should see a rheumatologist who might be familiar with my condition, but it was extremely difficult to get an appointment, so I asked Dr. Meyer and Dr. Jones to help me navigate the Ochsner system to set up an appointment. Almost immediately, they were successful, and appointment dates opened up.

One of the doctors I had seen thus far (I truly don't remember which one) recommended that I get a nerve conduction test to identify any nerve damage I might have that was causing or contributing to my worsening condition. With the help of my doctors, I was able to schedule the test for November 6. When I arrived at Ochsner Baptist Hospital for the test, I met Dr. Greenwald, a specialist in electrodiagnostic medicine, who said he was one of only twenty doctors in all of Louisiana who could administer the nerve conduction test and that I should thank my doctors for "pulling strings" to get me an appointment—which, of course, I did!

During the nerve test, electric impulses are sent through different areas to determine how quickly your nerves react to them. This helps identify areas of nerve damage. When the test was completed, Dr. Greenwald had a consultation with me about the results. He said he had been looking at the results of my other tests in my chart and now, with the results of the nerve test, he had an idea of what was causing my condition. I was stunned. Dr. Greenwald was the sixth doctor I had seen since August, and he was the first to offer a possible diagnosis.

He said that while he was not a rheumatologist or an arthritis specialist, he'd had other patients with similar symptoms, and he offered his opinion that I had a condition called PMR. What? I thought. Is that a form of cancer?

Dr. Greenwald provided me with some reading material on PMR, which is short for polymyalgia rheumatica. This is a condition that involves the body experiencing widespread aching and stiffness, much like the worst arthritis or rheumatism you can imagine. It sometimes goes hand in hand with an autoimmune disease called giant cell arteritis. PMR's cause is unknown, and it is hard to diagnose. But the written description of my condition closely mirrored what I was feeling. I had not yet been able to see a rheumatologist, but this neurologist seemed to hit it on the nose.

Meanwhile, I had a CAT scan of my chest and abdomen to further rule out any other possibilities.

I called Dr. Meyer later that day to tell her what Dr. Greenwald had suggested was the cause of my condition. She knew that steroids (prednisone) were the common treatment, and she prescribed a steroid pack as an intermediate treatment to give me some relief while I waited for a rheumatology appointment. She called in a prescription for methylprednisolone tablets, which I filled, and the next day, I felt immediate relief. In the morning, after taking the first dose, I called to my wife to come downstairs right away. She rushed down, figuring something terrible had happened, only to witness me getting out of a chair with little effort, something I hadn't been able to do for several months. Honestly, it felt like a miracle.

A couple days later, I finally got to see the Ochsner rheumatologists, Dr. Chandana Keshavamurthy and Dr. Alexandria Reese, my seventh and eighth doctors. (When I first asked to see a rheumatologist, I was told it would not be until March or April 2024, and I was so desperate to see someone who might help me that I contacted a rheumatologist outside of the Ochsner system, Dr. Austin Fraser with the Rheumatology Group.

After a blood workup, he told me he believed the PMR diagnosis was correct. He also felt it would be better for me to stay in the Ochsner system since they had all my records. He was, however, my ninth doctor!)

When I did get to see Drs. Keshavamurthy and Reese, they confirmed the PMR diagnosis and put me on a regular steroid program that would last almost a year. After the steroids had alleviated my condition, the prescribed treatment program I approved involved tapering off the steroids throughout 2024.

Naturally, steroids can have side effects, including high blood pressure, cataracts, bone loss, and thinning of the skin. To get a baseline against which to measure the steroid's effects, I had another MRI, X-rays of my neck and spine, and an ultrasound of my thyroid. I was also sent to an ophthalmologist, Dr. Nelson, my tenth doctor, who confirmed that my cataracts were minor and not a cause for concern at this time.

The ultrasound detected several nodules on my thyroid, so I was sent to an endocrinologist, whom I was able to see in February 2024. In consultation with Dr. Swarna Rai, my eleventh doctor, we will do an ultrasound every six months to see if further tests are warranted.

I had additional lab work and a bone density test for the baseline. Because continual use of steroids can weaken your bones, Dr. Reese prescribed Fosamax, a drug that builds bone density. So I took a medication (prednisone) that weakens my bones and then a medication (Fosamax) to build up my bones! Such is the weird world of medicine.

After I taper off the steroids, there is a slight possibility the PMR could reappear, and in that case, I will have to go back on some type of steroid program, since it has been shown that nonsteroidal and other anti-inflammatory drugs are not an effective treatment for PMR. But so far so good, so I am hopeful.

The polymyalgia rheumatica upended my life (I had two MRIs, one CAT scan, one ultrasound, four laboratory blood workups, a nerve conduction test, a bone density test, and several X-rays on the way to a diagnosis of my condition). I contemplated what life would be like if my condition could not be treated. Polymyalgia rheumatica is most common in people over fifty, so if you are in that category and suddenly begin to experience aches and pains like you've never experienced before, keep in mind that PMR could be the problem.

Postscript: You may be wondering why I've talked about only eleven doctors when the title of the story says "thirteen." In early 2024, I had two caps in my teeth fall out, so I had to see my dentist and an oral surgeon—my twelfth and thirteenth doctors in eight months. I'm sure others have seen more, but thirteen is plenty for me!

Postscript No. 2: At the end of 2024, when I was completing my steroid program, I found out that I needed my right hip replaced. It would go along with my left hip, which was replaced in 2021. In November 2024, I had it replaced, and two months later, I had my final appointment with the rheumatologists to celebrate the end of my PMR treatment. At the appointment, I asked if I should continue with the Fosamax bone treatment. The rheumatologists said that they had put me on the bone builder primarily because the bone scan revealed I had weak bones in my hips, but now that I'd had both of my hips replaced, there was no need to build my bones back up with the Fosamax!

Aviophobia: For those of you who aren't keeping up with your phobias, aviophobia is the fear of flying, which affects less than 3 percent of the population—including me. I think there are two different ways you develop aviophobia. One is to have a singular traumatic experience like having the door fly off the plane while in flight or watching the engine catch fire from your seat. The second is having a series of bad or troubling experiences that, when added up, cause you to never want to fly again. I think I suffer from the latter.

You've already read about a few of my troubled flights, including the blizzard in Denver, nearly crashing in Indonesia, and flying over a typhoon in the South China Sea. Here are a few of my other flying experiences.

Let's Go to Jackson

In 1988, I had been the New Orleans city planning director for seven years, and during that time, I had increased the staff, helped plan the 1984 World's Fair, and hired excellent young planners to carry out the mission of my agency. However, New Orleans had fallen on hard financial times, and the mayor and city council were forced to cut the city's budget, which meant that most agencies were called on to cut their staff and salary increases were put on hold. The process of laying off talented staff whom I had just hired was very unappealing, and not being able to count on any increase in my salary was distressing. I began to look for another position.

One potential opportunity that held interest for me was a job as director of the Hillsborough County Planning Commission in Tampa, Florida. It would be a promotion, since Hillsborough County was experiencing rapid population growth and the salary they were offering was significantly higher than what I was making at the time. I applied and was excited when I was invited to fly to Tampa to interview for the position. I interviewed in the morning and was invited back in the afternoon for a second round. Unfortunately, however, I was told that they'd offered the position to another candidate, so I boarded a plane in the evening to fly back to New Orleans.

If you've ever flown into or out of Tampa, you know that the city is famous for rain and lightning storms. After we left Tampa, I looked out my window and saw the sky light up with lightning as we flew over the Gulf of Mexico. When the lightning flashed, I could see rain splashing against the wings and engine as the plane flew the five hundred miles to New Orleans in turbulent weather.

The closer we got to New Orleans, the worse the weather became, and it was clear that this storm pattern existed across the Gulf South. Service on the flight was canceled, and the stewardesses moved down the aisle making sure everyone had their seat belts firmly buckled. I was not a happy camper and prayed for us to land and the flight to be over.

As we approached Armstrong International Airport, the captain came on and informed everyone that the weather in New Orleans was nasty and the landing would be bumpy. Since it was stormy, you could see nothing from the windows as we descended. Armstrong Airport is near the Mississippi River and has swamps and the river on one side and Lake Pontchartrain and the city and its suburbs on the other. Planes usually approached the runway from the north, either by crossing the lake and flying over the suburb of Kenner, or from the west, flying over swamps until they landed. Either way, it was a difficult landing even in the best of weather, so knowing that we were trying to land at night, in driving rain and wind, did not give me or any of the passengers confidence.

We dove through the clouds, and I could barely make out the city as the plane rocked and rolled toward the airport. Suddenly, the pilot gunned the engines, and the plane pulled up into a steep climb—the pilot having determined he'd misjudged the runway and needed to make a second try at landing. There were lots of gasps and moaning as people realized we were going to have to climb, turn around, and make a return to try again. The turbulence seemed to be getting more severe as we felt the plane bank to the right and make a long sweep to get into position to line up the runway.

We tried again, back down through the clouds into worsening wind and rain. The plane was bouncing and swaying back and forth against the wind. You could hardly make out the ground as the rain pelted against the windows. Sometimes the nose of the plane appeared to be rising and then plunging back down again as the pilot struggled to maintain the correct altitude while at the same time trying to find the runway. Suddenly, the plane shuddered; once again, the engines roared; and we began a very steep climb. After a few minutes, the plane leveled out above the clouds in the darkest of nights. Perhaps the pilots were trying to figure out what to do and whether they should make a third try at landing.

The captain came on the microphone once again. "As you can tell, we are having a little bit"—a little bit!—"of trouble maneuvering through the storm to the airport. We are going to try once more, so be sure your seat belts are buckled up and everyone, including the flight staff, is seated. If we can't make it this time, we may have to detour to Jackson, Mississippi, to land."

Almost immediately, a cry went up from what seemed like everyone on the plane: "Let's go to Jackson!" The lady next to me, who had been white-knuckled since we left Tampa, shouted out, "For Christ's sake, go to Jackson!"

The plane began descending, so we all knew the pilots were going to give it one final try. Back we went through the clouds into the rain and wind. Down went the nose, and the plane shuddered as it was buffeted by the elements. Soon we could make out the ground as we dropped closer and closer. Finally, we heard the engines dial back, and we hit the runway once, bounced, and then hit it again before all the wheels connected with the ground. Slowly, we came to a complete stop—somewhere, I'm sure, close to the end of the runway. The plane then taxied back to the terminal and pulled up to the gate. The pilot came on once again. "We are sorry for the difficulty landing, and we appreciate your confidence in the crew. Welcome to New Orleans!"

Whereupon the lady next to me shouted out, "We should have gone to Jackson!"

Can a Raincoat Substitute for a Parachute?

In 2019, Pat and I flew to Ann Arbor, Michigan, to attend the christening of our latest grandchild, William, son of my daughter Amanda and her husband, Ben. Amanda met Ben Carlisle in graduate school at the University of Illinois at Chicago, in the urban planning program. Ben is from Ann Arbor, and after their marriage, they settled there, where Ben joined an urban planning firm founded by his father and Amanda became the executive director of the Washtenaw Housing Alliance, which focused on programs for the homeless. They already had two girls, Adeline and Georgia, and were now welcoming their son into the family.

By this time, I had already boarded the aviophobia train, so the prospect of a long flight to Ann Arbor did not appeal to me. But we found a direct flight to Detroit, where Amanda would pick us up and drive the fifty miles to Ann Arbor, and I had a Valium that my doctor had prescribed for me to "take the edge off," so I decided to make the trip.

A side note about Valium: The flight to Detroit was not the first time I was dependent on Valium. In 2015, I planned to travel to Iowa City, Iowa, to attend the fiftieth anniversary of the founding of the planning school I attended. To get to Iowa City, you flew to Dallas Fort Worth and then took a regional carrier to Cedar Rapids and a car to Iowa City. I was nervous about making the trip, so I went to see my primary physician, who advised taking Valium for the journey. When I got to the airport in New Orleans, I was really feeling anxious, so I thought, Why not take two of the pills? If one would take the edge off, two should make for an even more pleasant flight!

The flight from New Orleans to Dallas was great. When the plane arrived at DFW airport, I had to be awakened by a flight attendant, and I stumbled out of the plane, trying to determine how I would find my connecting flight in that large airport. I somehow realized that you had to take a monorail train to another terminal to get to the regional carrier. That terminal was located two terminals from the one I had just left, so I anticipated a short ride. I was still a bit groggy from the Valium, so after I boarded the monorail, I just held on to a strap and waited for the signal to announce I had arrived at Terminal C. Apparently, I missed the terminal and instead rode the train all the way around the airport until it returned to the original terminal from which I entered. Then the train made a second trip around the airport, with me oblivious to the fact that I was just riding the train and not getting off. Finally, a lady who'd gotten on the train with me earlier and was now returning from the terminal she'd originally gone to noticed that I was still on the same train and still hanging on to the same strap. She came over to me and asked if anything was wrong. I said I didn't think so and I was just waiting for the signal to exit to my new terminal. She said I had passed that up and offered to help me get off at the correct terminal, which she did and then pointed me to the right gate. If she had not intervened, I might still be going around and around on that train. Lesson? One Valium was enough!

The flight going up to Detroit was great, and we had a great visit celebrating William's christening. Going home was planned to be a repeat of the trip to Ann Arbor in reverse: my daughter would drive us back to Detroit, and then we would take a direct flight back to New Orleans. (I now look for every opportunity to either take a train or drive to whatever destination I'm going to. After Hurricane Katrina, I was invited to speak at a conference in Boston and took Amtrak from New Orleans to New York and then the Acela train to Boston. For the return trip, I took the Acela back to New York and boarded a train west to Chicago and then took Amtrak back to New Orleans.)

We had a morning flight from Detroit to New Orleans, and the weather was overcast with light rain. We got to Detroit in plenty of time, so I took my Valium, and we boarded the Delta flight for the nonstop trip to the Crescent City. Gradually, the pill took effect, and I settled in next to Pat for the two-and-a-half-hour flight. This isn't going to be so bad, I thought.

Somewhere around Nashville, I think, through the haze of the Valium, I began to hear various voices and movement in the cabin. I continued to doze until I noticed that the cabin seemed to be getting hotter. I opened one eye and muttered something to Pat about the plane being warmer than I anticipated. She said something must be wrong with the air-conditioning because the cabin was, in fact, getting much warmer. Slowly, I noticed the increasing chatter in the cabin and more passengers commenting on how warm it was getting. Then the pilot came on the microphone and said something like, "I'm sure many of you have noticed that the cabin has been getting warmer. We are having some difficulty with the air-conditioning controls, and hopefully we can rectify the situation shortly." That didn't happen, and it got warmer and warmer.

The pilot then said he was reducing altitude to alleviate the problem, and the plane began to descend quickly. After several minutes, the pilot said. "We are experiencing additional difficulties"—Additional difficulties? What difficulties?—"and we are detouring to Atlanta's Hartsfield Airport." Now, it didn't take a genius to know that there must be something more wrong with the plane than just the air-conditioning. The plane banked to the left, and we started on our way to Atlanta.

As more people realized what was happening, they began buzzing for the flight attendants to ask what was wrong and why we were going to Atlanta when we were so close to New Orleans. The flight attendants, who probably didn't know the nature of the problem, tried to reassure everyone that the detour was just a precaution and there would be another plane in Atlanta to take us to New Orleans.

After descending for twenty or thirty minutes, we began to see the ground very clearly and could make out specific buildings and traffic on the roadways. We got lower and lower. We were still at least half an hour from Atlanta but flying at an altitude usually experienced when a plane is about to land! It was almost a treetop flight! I was fully awake now, and both Pat and I looked at each other with some alarm. That same concern was fully on display with the rest of the passengers as we all wondered why we were flying so low for so long. One of the flight attendants walking down the aisle told the passenger in the seat ahead of me that the plane was experiencing mechanical difficulties but should reach the Atlanta airport safely. Mechanical difficulties! Reach the airport safely! What were those difficulties?

Pat tried to comfort me while other passengers put up a brave front, but everybody, I could see, looked upset. The pilot again came on the mike and told us that the plane was approaching the airport and that we were cleared to land. (Probably some emergency was declared and our plane was given priority to land.) As the wheels touched down, I could see emergency vehicles moving parallel with the plane in case they were needed. Fortunately, we came to a stop, and the pilot and crew began apologizing for having to land in Atlanta instead of New Orleans. We were just grateful to have landed!

We were given instructions to exit the plane, and when it got to be our turn to leave the cabin, I asked the flight attendant whether we were going to board a new plane for the trip to New Orleans. He responded, “I hope so.”

Pat said she was totally okay with renting a car for the trip to New Orleans if I was too upset to get on another plane. The airline, in fact, was offering vouchers for future travel if passengers did not wish to continue. I was upset, but perhaps it was the lingering effects of the Valium—I said no, I could make it on another plane. Thank goodness the weather was beautiful, so I was not concerned about a bumpy ride. We boarded a new plane and landed in New Orleans without incident. We never did discover what was wrong with the plane and how much danger we were actually in. But it was a very scary flight and made me think about how close we may have come to a tragic ending.

After we landed and made our way back home, Pat told me she was so scared on the flight that she contemplated taking radical action had the situation demanded it. She said she thought she could drag me to the front of the plane, force open the door, and jump with me, using her raincoat as a parachute. A raincoat as a parachute—you must be kidding me! Thank heavens it never came to that, since I'm pretty sure a raincoat would not substitute for a parachute.

The Christmas Adventure

In 2018, Pat and I made a quick trip to Dallas to spend Christmas with my daughter Jennifer and her family. On Southwest Airlines, the flight from New Orleans to Love Field is only about an hour and a half, so I thought that fortified with Valium, I could make the trip. We left a few days before Christmas and planned to return the day after.

The trip over went well, and we had a brief but wonderful holiday celebration. We were scheduled for a 1:30 p.m. flight back to New Orleans on December 26. That morning, the weather had turned awful, with heavy rain and howling wind. Jennifer said she would drive us to Love Field, and we left her house in plenty of time to get to the airport. Unfortunately, Jenny, apparently forgetting that Southwest flew out of its hub at Love Field, took us to the Dallas Fort Worth airport. As we approached the airport in torrential rain, I remarked that this did not look like the way to Love Field, whereupon Jennifer said, "Oh my God, I'm going to the wrong airport!" She turned around and made her way through afternoon traffic to Love Field.

When we arrived, we pulled in under cover to unload our luggage and stayed out of the horizontal wind spray as best we could. We said goodbye, took our luggage over to the outside baggage check-in, and made our way inside. I was already nervous seeing the weather we were going to have to take off in, and the car ride to the wrong airport didn't help matters much. We went through security, located our gate, and settled into our seats with a little bit of time left until our flight was scheduled to depart. As we sat in the terminal, the rain was splashing against the window with such force that you could hear it inside. The other planes and taxiways were almost invisible. I took my Valium and kept anxiously looking at the arrival/departure signage to see when we might be boarding the plane. The flight was delayed several times until it was nearly four o'clock. Just when I was convinced that the entire flight would be canceled and we would have to call our daughter to come back and pick us up to spend the night at her house (something I thought eminently reasonable given the terrible weather), the plane was called for boarding.

Everyone at the Southwest gate was looking at everyone else and saying we couldn't possibly be contemplating flying in this weather. But the gate attendants assured everyone we were, in fact, boarding the plane. As we reached the plane after going down the long access ramp, we noticed the plane was rocking in the wind and rain was seeping inside the protective covering designed to keep passengers dry until they were inside the plane. Frankly, I was terrified. There's no way we can take off in this weather, I assured myself. I'm sure every other passenger had the same thought. We settled in and put our seat belts on, and the flight attendants asked if anyone would like beverage service now before we took off, figuring that the bad weather would make in-flight service impossible.

My wife was sitting in an aisle seat, while I was in the middle seat, and a young man had the window seat. We talked, and I learned he was from England, on holiday in the United States. He had been to Las Vegas and then traveled to Dallas. He told us that he was going to spend a few days in New Orleans and then travel to Miami before flying home. We suggested a few restaurants he could try in and around the French Quarter and a few attractions he should visit.

The pilot came on and said we were holding at the gate until there was a break in the weather and other flights ahead of us could clear the runway. I was good with holding at the gate! We stayed there for at least an hour. Dusk started to fall. There was no break in the weather; it was still windy and pouring rain. Finally, the pilot said we were cleared to leave the gate and move out onto the taxiway. No way! I thought. But off we went and slowly made our way out to the taxiway, where we could see ten or so planes lined up ahead of us. We stopped and waited another forty-five minutes on the tarmac while our plane rocked in the wind.

I kept looking out the window to see if I could see any light in the clouds. Then I noticed the first plane in line turn and motor back to the terminal. Then a few more planes returned to their gate, and a few more, until all the planes ahead of us had turned back, leaving us as the number one option to take off. We moved out to the runway and sat at the end, ready to go. At this point, I noticed that our new friend sitting next to us was putting on an eye shade that covered both eyes. He noticed me looking at him and remarked, "I don't like flying anytime, and I don't want to see anything when we take off!"

We waited and then we waited some more until I was convinced that the pilot would not be given the signal to take off—surely no air traffic controller would give that command in the horrendous weather we continued to experience.

Suddenly, the pilot came on and said, "We are cleared for takeoff!" He gunned the engine, and the plane rolled down the runway, picking up speed. Even though all the wheels were still on the ground, we could feel the plane being pushed from side to side in the wind. It was white-knuckle time for everyone. When the plane reached the appropriate speed, the pilot pulled the nose up, and we made a rapid ascent. Not a gradual assent—a rapid ascent. The plane was clearly fighting the wind, and it groaned (at least it seemed to me to groan!) as it rose rapidly, the pilot trying to get above the rain clouds as quickly as possible. It was night, and no lights could be seen, so it was impossible to get any sense of where we were or what was happening—except that the nose continued to point up and we were all pinned against our seats.

After what seemed an eternity, the plane leveled off, and although it was still being buffeted by the wind and rain, I felt encouraged that we could make the short trip to New Orleans—although I wondered why I hadn't taken two Valiums back at the airport.

After about twenty minutes, the pilot came on the mike and said, "You may have noticed that there is a lot of heavy weather on our trip to New Orleans"—"heavy weather" being a dramatic understatement! "We're going to try and fly around the weather, so we're detouring up to Memphis, and then we will swing around and try coming in to New Orleans from the east. Hopefully, we will encounter better weather. Of course, this is going to add significant time to our flight, and I will keep you informed of our anticipated ETA."

For me, this was the worst of all situations. The fact that we were adding a major amount of time in the air was not something I wanted to hear, and I knew the announcement would make Pat and the other passengers nervous as well. My friend next to me still had his mask on, so I don't know if he was faking sleep or if he heard the announcement. Whatever the case, I was not going to disturb him as he was better off in his oblivious state.

We could feel the plane bank to the left as it turned toward Memphis. When we had reached either Memphis or the limit of the really bad weather, it turned right for about thirty minutes and moved south toward the Gulf Coast. The weather, while still rough, was nothing like what we left behind in Dallas. Another hour or so and the pilot announced we were cleared to land in New Orleans.

It was close to midnight when we landed. We exited the plane, thanked the flight attendants for their assistance on what had been a horrible flight, and made our way to the baggage claim area. Everyone was talking about how they would never fly again or wondering if they could still rent a car at this late hour. My friend met us in baggage claim and said he was going to try to get a cab downtown. We offered to give him a ride, but he declined. We all waited by the conveyor belt for our luggage. After fifteen minutes or so, no baggage was on the belts, and several of us went over to the Southwest ticket office, which was closed, except for one porter who was waiting for the luggage as well. Finally, someone in a Southwest uniform came toward the crowd and said, "Folks, I'm sorry to tell you that your plane left Dallas without your baggage. We will put your bags on the next flight tomorrow morning and let everyone know when it arrives." Pat and I drove home and immediately went to bed. What a fitting end to our flight!

Atlantic City

By the late 1980s, the city was convinced that the Louisiana legislature would legalize casino gambling, beginning with gaming on riverboats and featuring one land-based casino in New Orleans. If the lawmakers passed enabling legislation for a single casino in the city, it would fall to the local unit of government to determine the parameters under which the casino would be built and operated. We had limited understanding of the impacts of casino gaming and thus were at a disadvantage in trying to draft zoning and other tools to regulate a casino's operation. Other than Nevada, the latest city to implement gambling as an economic development tool at the time was Atlantic City, New Jersey, which was in such desperate shape that it seized on gambling to spur development. Despite the opposition to casino gambling from various groups on moral grounds, Atlantic City moved quickly to implement land-based casino gaming. In 1974, New Jersey voted against legalizing casino gambling statewide but two years later approved a new referendum that legalized casinos but restricted them to Atlantic City. The first casino opened in 1978, and several others followed in the '80s.

New Orleans organized a trip to Atlantic City to see what we could learn from their experience. In January 1986, several New Orleans officials traveled to Atlantic City, including myself from the planning commission, Karen Milner from the city attorney's office, and a representative of the chief administrative office. We flew from New Orleans to Philadelphia and then transferred to a smaller airplane for the short trip to Atlantic City. The weather was bad in Philadelphia, with snow and plenty of wind, and the smaller plane probably had only eight or ten seats. I recall that we had to board the plane from the tarmac, and the interior was small. How small, you ask? A curtain separated the pilot from the passengers!

The ride was very bumpy. One of the passengers inquired if there was any in-flight beverage service. There were no flight attendants on the flight, so I was sure there was going to be no food or drink provided. However, after we'd been aloft for a few minutes, the pilot stuck his head through the curtain and pointed to a cooler on the floor, which contained some drinks. I'm not sure any alcoholic beverages were present, but we could have used some. As the flight got rougher, I shouted to the pilot over the roar of the engine, seeking some clarification about our trip. Finally, the pilot reached around the curtain and said something unintelligible that no one could understand. It seemed he spoke no English, so all we could do was hold on for dear life. After landing, went to our hotel; Karen remembers that her room had a mirrored ceiling. Casino gaming, here we come!

Our meetings with the mayor and other officials went well, and we returned to New Orleans with a lot of information. Land-based casino gambling was sold to the people of Louisiana as a Monte Carlo stand-alone model with minimal amenities, no attached hotel, and a small restaurant. This was to be sure that the benefits of the casino would accrue not just to the national casino operator but also to local hotels, restaurants, and entertainment venue owners. Our rules reflected this intent as well as regulating the size and design of the building. Most of the casino gambling approved in the early 1990s elsewhere in Louisiana was designed to be operated on riverboats, reflecting the historical and idealized operation of gaming in the age of the riverboat. Originally, the number of boats was limited to fifteen, and there were restrictions that required the boats to sail on the water.

However, once the gaming industry got its foot in the door and hired an army of lobbyists, gradually, over the years, virtually all the restrictions were lifted. Riverboats were permitted to operate tied to the land since they earned far more money when they were not sailing and were stationed at the dock. The land-based casino (which became Harrah's Casino and is now Caesars) was eventually allowed to have an associated hotel and then a variety of restaurants and entertainment venues on-site. So dependent has the state become on casino gaming, the lottery, sports betting, and a horse racing track with video poker and slot machines that all forms of gaming now account for around 10 percent of the state's operating budget.

Clearly, the lessons we learned from our trip to Atlantic City and the rules and regulations we formulated from those lessons were no match for the casino industry and the desire of the state and city to generate revenue while not raising taxes.

ATMs

Perhaps when the Singularity comes, there will be no need for ATMs. I hope so, because if you are anything like me, they consistently confound you. They are constantly broken, or they don't have money in the denominations you want, or they can't change the language from Spanish to English, or they want to know if you want an auto loan before they give you your money—or any number of excuses, when you're just trying to get $100 out of your account. The following are a couple of examples of my experiences with ATMs.

Backing Out of the Drive-Through

We all know how the drive-through ATM works. You drive up to a dispensing machine, which is usually embedded in the bank building wall and next to one or more drive-through lanes, where you put your paper information into a pneumatic tube that sends it to a teller with whom you communicate through a speaker box and, often, a small television screen. If you're in the ATM lane, you put your card in the slot, punch in your PIN, and carry out your business. When you're in that lane, there is nowhere to go but forward as other customers are usually pulling in behind you waiting for you to complete your transaction so they can pull up and begin their interaction with the machine.

One day, I was going to my local bank's ATM and pulled in behind a car that was already at the machine. Almost immediately, one and then two other cars pulled in behind me. I waited for the driver in front of me to complete their business so they could pull forward and leave and I could take their place. But nothing happened, and it was apparent that the woman in the car was having problems with the machine. Usually, when this happens, a little time goes by, the driver gets frustrated or angry and decides to leave, and the situation resolves itself. But for some unknown reason, this woman decided she needed to back up. That was not an option: my car was there, and even if I'd wanted to accommodate her, I couldn't have, because there were two other cars behind me. When she started beeping for me to back up, the cars behind me began beeping for her to pull forward and leave. Then she decided to squeeze out of her driver side door and motion for me to back up. So I yelled (okay, maybe it wasn't a yell, but it was more than a polite conversation!) that she needed to move forward—whereupon she said that for some reason, she couldn't put her car in gear to go forward. Now there was nothing but beeping from the cars that were already behind me and several more that had entered the line.

Fortunately, a woman in the passenger seat of the car behind me got out, went over to the woman at the ATM, and helped her get her car in gear. We all felt relieved—until the woman began to pull forward but was so flustered that she jumped a protective curb, hit one of the concrete poles the bank had installed to prevent cars from hitting the building, and stalled out of her car. Now no one could get out. Several of us went over to her, put her car in neutral, and pushed it out of the lane and into a space on the street while she went into the bank to report the accident with the poles. And that's how a five-minute trip to the ATM turns into a twenty-minute adventure.

How Do You Operate This Thing?

During the COVID-19 pandemic, most banks closed their lobby areas to customers, forcing everyone to use the ATM or the drive-through teller. For everyone who had only to make a simple transaction, this may have presented an inconvenience, but it wasn't a hardship. However, if you had more complicated business, it could be a real hassle.

It so happened that one day I had to go the bank to deposit a check and pulled in behind a lady who had just pulled in front of me in a large sedan. After a few minutes of nothing happening, I could see that the woman was having a conversation with the teller, who, of course, was inside the bank. I overheard some of the conversation, which went something like this:

"Where is the container you want me to put my deposit slip in?" the woman said.

"You must open the door and take out the container. Then put your slip and money inside, close the container, put it back in the compartment, close the compartment, and press the send button," the teller said.

"How do I open the door?" she inquired.

"Just open the door, which you can reach from your driver's seat," said the teller, becoming exasperated.

I could see the woman trying to reach through to get the canister; finally, she succeeded in pulling it inside her car. "Now what do I do?"

"Fill out a deposit slip or a withdrawal slip, put it in the canister, and send it back to me."

There was a long pause. Then the woman said, "I don't know how to do that. When I come to the bank, I always go inside, and a teller helps me to fill out the forms. This is the first time I have ever been to an outside window."

I began to realize that the woman—who, as you probably can guess, was somewhat elderly—had never been to a drive-through window, and when she went to the bank she always went inside and got help from the bank staff. Now that she couldn't go into the bank and was forced to use the outside drive-through, she was completely bewildered. I got out of my car, went over to her, and explained her situation to the teller over the microphone. I said to the image on the television screen, "You need to help her, or we'll be here all day." The teller, finally appreciating the situation, told the lady to park her car and he would come down and help her—which he did, face mask and all.

Animal Adventures

"Like a true nature's child
We were born, born to be wild"
—"Born to Be Wild," Steppenwolf

Most, but not all, of my animal stories occurred while I was with the Audubon Zoo. Working at the zoo was a wonderful opportunity to interact with all manner of animals and learn about their habits, environment, food, capabilities, and health—not something a city planner normally experiences. Here are a few zoo stories plus some other animal adventures.

Medical Care: Garth and Gators

I know what you're thinking, but sorry, this story is not about Garth Brooks! It's a story about how I was pressed into service to help the zoo staff with alligators and a large lion called Garth.

One of the great perks of working in a zoo is having the opportunity to go behind the scenes to see how the curators and keepers go about taking care of their charges. There is so much involved in exhibiting animals that the public is simply not aware of, including preparing the proper diets, feeding the animals well, and being sure there are enrichment programs for the

animals that benefit from them. Keepers also prepare and repair the exhibits themselves, including installing appropriate landscaping and designing educational signage. Keepers daily examine the restraints that keep particularly dangerous animals contained, including glass viewing areas, piano wire exhibits, and simulated rock enclosures.

But my most enjoyable experiences at the zoo involved the medical care of the animals. All zoo animals have yearly comprehensive physicals as well as having their behavior constantly monitored to be sure adverse medical conditions are caught early enough to be treated. Most medical treatment is administered and supervised by zoo veterinarians, but sometimes other specialists are called in, such as dentists or specialists in exotic diseases. Medical examinations are routine events for the animal staff but are very special occasions for the non-animal staff, and office staff were always hopeful of being invited to watch medical treatments being administered and sometimes actually participate in the examinations.

One of my more memorable participations in a medical exam occurred when the staff of our swamp exhibit asked if I would like to see them catch an alligator for its annual physical. How exciting, I thought. Our swamp exhibit featured multiple alligators, including some who were more than ten feet in length—that's a big gator. I went to the exhibit and watched the keepers gather and identify a particularly big animal, which was the subject of the day's activities. Alligators like to rest on the banks of lagoons, and our exhibit was designed to highlight that activity by providing plenty of opportunity for the gators to bask in the sun while visitors observed their activity from the safety of raised boardwalks.

That is where I positioned myself to get a good view of how the animal staff would corral this large animal. As I leaned against the guardrail overlooking the exhibit, the swamp exhibit curator called out to me, "Bob, come on around and hop over the guardrail and join us in the exhibit." A ten-foot or better alligator is nothing to fool around with, and I wondered why I would be invited to get into the exhibit with the staff and a large alligator. Soon I understood. In order to restrain the alligator, seven or eight of the staff (men and women) would jump on top of him, using their combined weight to hold the animal down while another staff member taped his mouth shut and other staff members pulled his legs up behind him to keep him from just rising up and walking away. Other staff would jump on his tail, which can be a formidable weapon.

I thought, This is nuts! We were all going to jump on a big gator and try to hold him down while other members of the staff immobilized his mouth, legs, and tail. The keepers explained that the anesthetic that is used on mammals can't be used on reptiles, so it was necessary to physically restrain the animal.

How would we do this without the alligator turning on us? It turned out that one keeper would try to get the alligator's attention while the other staff snuck up alongside and prepared to jump on him. Feeling very unprepared for this adventure, I lined up with several of the keepers on one side while a similar number lined up on the other. A rope loop was gingerly draped over the alligator's mouth and tightened to close it, providing some measure of protection before the animal was completely immobilized. Then, when the swamp curator felt the time was right and the animal was distracted, he yelled "Now!" and we all leaped on this ten-foot monster. Our combined weight was well over one thousand pounds, but the animal seemed not to be too impressed as he raised himself on his legs and started forward.

Two people grabbed his legs and pulled them back, causing him to fall on his stomach, in which position his mouth could be taped shut. Someone then put a bag over his head to disorient him, and the veterinarians began their examination. That was my first and last time jumping on an alligator.

The other zoo medical story that stands out in my mind concerns our Asian lion, Garth. When it was time for Garth's annual physical, the mammal staff asked me if I would like to observe. Once again, I jumped at the chance, and the fact that this examination was going to be performed on one of the largest mammals in the animal kingdom made it extra special. On a Wednesday morning, I was directed over to the animal hospital, where I waited for Garth to be brought over from the night house attached to his exhibit.

You don't just put a collar on a four-hundred-pound male lion and walk him over to the doctor's office for his physical. The veterinary staff would have to administer a sedative and wait for it to take effect. Then Garth would be put on a heavy-duty gurney, loaded on the back of a truck, and brought over to the animal hospital. Around eight thirty in the morning, the truck pulled up to the back of the hospital with Garth inside. The first order of business would be to take his weight so it could be compared to the previous year's weight as one indicator of the animal's overall health.

Once again, you don't just ask a lion if he'll stand on a scale so his weight can be taken. And you don't use a typical household scale to hold an enormous lion. While I watched, a team of keepers offloaded the gurney, carried Garth into the courtyard of the hospital, and placed him on a large custom-made scale that was used to weigh our bears, our primates, and our collection of cats, including jaguars, tigers, leopards, and lions. I was fascinated watching the medical team take up their positions to draw blood, examine legs and paws, and inspect teeth as well as eyes and ears. The anesthetic basically paralyzed the animal while not putting him to sleep. I learned that whenever possible, the veterinarians preferred to simply immobilize animals as opposed to having them lose consciousness—for the same reason doctors avoid a general anesthetic when a local one can achieve the same goal.

As the staff positioned Garth on the scale, it became clear that he could not completely fit on it—he was so long that both his head and part of his rear end were falling off. One of the staff who was attempting to settle him motioned to me. "Bob, can you come over here and hold his head so it doesn't fall down? That could hurt his breathing." My first reaction was that this must be a joke the animal staff was playing on the guy from the front office. But the keeper reiterated quickly, "Get over here and support his head!" This was more adventure that I'd bargained for, but I made my way over to the scale. Garth's head must have weighed thirty pounds all by itself and was so large you could not simply hold it up it a standing position. You had to get on the ground and hold the head in your lap!

Several of the keepers helped me get into position, and I slid myself, on my knees, under his head until it rested on my lap. Garth was breathing heavily and staring straight at me. His mouth was open, and he slobbered all over me. Those teeth were just about the most frightening thing I'd ever witnessed. I was sure he was trying to figure out how to neutralize the anesthetic so he could grab my head in his mouth. As the staff began their examination, it was not lost on me that I was the only person sitting on the ground and that it would not be easy to extract myself from that position should the need arise. The curator of mammals, Roger Isles, was standing near the staff, holding a shotgun. As Roger later explained to me, it was standard procedure for a member of the zoo's shooting team to be armed when medical examinations of potentially dangerous mammals were being conducted, just in case the animal unexpectedly came out of the anesthetic and decided it wanted to be elsewhere. How come nobody told me about this possibility before?

The keepers have a game they frequently play during these examinations called guess the animal's weight. They try to guess the weight of the animal on the scale, and the keeper closest to its actual weight gets a prize at the end of the day, usually at a local beer joint. I could see the keepers taking turns guessing Garth's weight as the vets adjusted the scale, and I could see the surprised look on their faces when it turned out Garth weighed considerably more than any of them had guessed. Later on, I learned that the amount of anesthetic used is based roughly on the weight of the animal. More weight, more anesthetic—seems reasonable to me. So the fact that Garth weighed more than anyone guessed brought the amount of anesthetic administered into question. I was oblivious to this concern. I was just concerned about this enormous animal looking longingly at me! Garth seemed to me to be moving a little too much, and one of the veterinarians decided to quickly add to the anesthetic dose originally applied. Garth let out a low growl and lifted his head slightly. I was frozen, stone-cold inert. I couldn't move. If the lion decided to get up or become aggressive, there was absolutely nothing I could do. I couldn't run—hell, I couldn't even stand. I would have been a goner. But Garth settled back down with the additional sedative, and one of the keepers brought over a low stool to support his head, telling me I could shift his head to the stool and stand up.

I tried to maneuver out from under Garth's head while a keeper shifted the stool to hold its weight. I had to have help in standing up, and when I did, everyone noticed that I had wet my pants! Hey, you would too, if you were holding up the head of a four-hundred-pound lion and realized there was no escape for you if something went wrong. I excused myself from the rest of the medical procedures and went back to my office, a little embarrassed but thrilled I was still alive.

The Warthog

It's not common knowledge except in the zoo profession, but animals escape their enclosures all the time. Most of the time, the animals involved are not dangerous (think birds), or if they do escape from their primary enclosure, they are contained by secondary barriers. Out of a collection of thousands of animals, I estimate that about one hundred or so would be dangerous should they escape. For these animals, escapes are rare, but they do happen.

So it was when the zoo received an African warthog from another zoo, which Audubon was preparing to put on exhibit. African warthogs are members of the pig family and are found in grassland, savanna, and woodland areas in sub-Saharan Africa. They are short, squat animals with two pairs of tusks protruding from the mouth and curving upward. The tusks are not used for digging but for defense against predators and combat with other warthogs. They can inflict very severe injuries if you are gored. A fully grown warthog can weigh over three hundred pounds and is an extremely powerful animal. They live in groups, so exhibiting them usually involves more than one. The animal Audubon received was to be the first of several that would make up a group in the exhibit.

On the day the warthog was to be delivered, staff prepared a temporary holding area behind its main exhibit, so it was isolated from other zoo animals while it underwent a period of quarantine. The temporary enclosure was a heavy-gauge chain-link fence and backed up to the concrete block night house, which would provide weather protection for the animal should it rain. A typical quarantine period would last several weeks until the staff felt comfortable that the warthog would adjust well to its temporary home and could be transferred to the permanent exhibit.

A truck from the zoo that was lending the animal arrived with the warthog in a crate. Roger Isles, the zoo's curator of mammals, oversaw offloading the crate, getting it inside the chain-link enclosure, and setting the animal free to explore its temporary home. Because of the warthog's weight, a forklift was used to take the crate off the truck, and then the warthog was muscled into the enclosure by the animal staff. Roger then opened the crate's door, and the warthog walked out calmly into the enclosure. The staff gathered around the fence to observe what is an unusual-looking animal, one that had not previously been exhibited at our zoo.

After patrolling the perimeter, the warthog apparently decided he did not like his new home and took off running right into a part of the fence enclosure. But one run was not enough, and after the animal had bounced off the fence, he retreated across the enclosure and again ran and rammed into the same part of the fence he'd previously hit. Now, a three-hundred-pound pig running at full speed across fifty or sixty feet of space generates quite an impact, but the warthog was not phased at all. The staff did not seem concerned; they had experience with other animals who, on entering a new space, often ran into fences as they searched for a way to escape.

The warthog also did not seem concerned that he might hurt himself running full speed into the fence, so he repeated his dash to freedom again—and again and again. In fact, Roger was becoming concerned that eventually he might hurt himself, so he made efforts to distract the pig with food and snacks. But the warthog was having none of it and continued running into the fence at full speed. This might not have been a problem; however, the staff noticed that the constant bombardment was beginning to pull the metal posts out of the ground. In fact, it became clear that it was not going to take long before an entire length of fence came detached and the animal was loose along a back service road.

Nonessential staff and observers were ordered out of the area as a precaution. A loose hog would be extremely dangerous and could not be allowed to gain access to any public area. Roger ordered up a backhoe, which had a bucket on the front and was normally used to transport sand or dirt. We then scrambled to find a large piece of plywood we could attach to the bucket. We hoped to use this makeshift device to herd or push the warthog back from the fence and, hopefully, into the concrete night house, which would contain our upset pig. After staff tied the plywood to the bucket, Roger jumped into the backhoe just as the warthog pushed over the battered fence. Before he could escape, the backhoe with the attached plywood pushed back against him. The veterinary staff stood by with a tranquilizer gun to immobilize the hog should he escape as well as a shotgun should it be necessary to take more severe action to prevent anyone from being harmed.

The pig was startled by the plywood and the sound of the backhoe. He looked confused and moved back as the backhoe moved forward. Then the hog decided he would take on the backhoe directly. As opposed to trying to go around the plywood, he began running and hitting it directly, just as he had done to the fence. The keepers yelled to Roger that he had to speed up the process before the warthog realized there was an easier way around the backhoe to freedom. The backhoe sped up, but the pig kept up the attack. Then we heard the plywood crack under the force of the relentless hammering. Thankfully, the pig backed into the night house, and while the plywood held him inside, the keepers managed to shut and lock the door. Everyone breathed a sigh of relief that the animal was safely contained and no one was hurt. But we now knew that any new chain-link enclosure that was designed to hold such a powerful and single-minded animal had to be built much more securely—a lesson in pig power!

Lagniappe: The prominent computer engineer and futurist Ray Kurzweil has predicted society will reach the Singularity by 2045, approximately twenty years from now. Don't confuse the Singularity with the totality of eclipse fame. The Singularity is the point at which artificial intelligence and machine learning will surpass human intelligence and human society will be unable to control the machines. Does that mean we will have to be on the lookout for the Terminator?

Zoo School

While the keepers, curators, and veterinary staff know a great deal about the animals under their charge, the rest of the staff of a typical zoo—the managers in marketing, visitor services, maintenance, construction, development, operations, and so on—know next to nothing about them. The profession has developed a specialized school to offer a variety of training programs about the zoo profession to address this problem. One program offered for the nonanimal staff is zoo biology for nonbiologists. This program offers multiday classes in biology and the classification and characteristics of animals typically found in zoo collections. I was given the opportunity to attend this program, and I eagerly accepted. The school is held in Ogilvie Park, West Virginia, near Wheeling, West Virginia, and the session I attended was held in the winter. Normally, traveling north in the winter is not something I would look forward to, but this was a learning opportunity I couldn't pass up.

The "campus" at Oglebay Resort and Conference Center consists of a twenty-thousand-square-foot business center surrounded by a hotel with 250 rooms and a wide variety of amenities, including several restaurants, a fitness center, an indoor pool, and a golf course, all located in a beautiful rural area with hiking and biking trails. In the winter, with snow on the ground, it is a magical environment.

My class contained about forty individuals from zoos across the country. They were all part of the nonanimal staff and very eager to fill in gaps in their biological knowledge. It was a very impressive group. The instructors were all experienced zoo managers with extensive knowledge of the biology of the animals they cared for and were enthusiastic and entertaining.

One day, after classes ended, I decided to walk down to a small lake at the foot of a large hill where the conference center is located. I was in a business suit with dress shoes, and the weather was chilly, but I thought I would walk down to the lake, spend a few minutes there, and then go back up the hill to the hotel. As I walked down, it began to snow, and I saw several deer gathering at the bottom of the hill. It was idyllic. I had noticed that the walkway was frozen over in several places, but I was able to make my way down the hill and really didn't think much more about it. I lost track of time, and after a while, I began to realize that I was getting cold and that the light snow had turned into a blizzard, completely obscuring the top of the hill and covering the already frozen ground.

I tried to walk back up the hill but could not find the path under the snow. I attempted to make my own path up the hill, but in my dress shoes, I kept sliding back to the base of the hill. After numerous attempts, it dawned on me that if I couldn't get back up the hill, I might freeze to death during zoo school! In desperation, I took off my shoes and crawled back up the hill on my hands and knees. When I got to the top, the knees of my suit pants were torn, and I was flushed from the effort—not to mention my socks, which were completely soaked. I looked like a homeless person who had been given an old suit. I had to pass several areas where other school attendees were standing waiting for dinner and did my best to explain my appearance. I was the talk of the school that day and probably did not present the best image of professionalism. The lesson: Don't go to Western Pennsylvania in the winter!

The Green Mamba

Most zoos have buildings dedicated to the exhibition of reptiles, including lizards, snakes, and crocodilians. Dedicated buildings are preferred, not only because reptiles are extremely sensitive to changes in temperature, requiring enclosures that allow the temperature to be tightly controlled, but also because some species are dangerous and their exhibits require strict security. Audubon Zoo has such a facility, which allows a large variety of reptiles to be exhibited, including snakes. While many types of snakes are not poisonous or constrictors of some type, it is the poisonous ones that are generally the most interesting to zoo visitors.

Among the snakes in Audubon's collection were a variety of poisonous ones, including rattlesnakes from the Southwest, snakes from Louisiana such as the cottonmouth and copperhead, vipers such as the Gaboon viper, and cobras, including the king cobra. Also included in the collection were snakes from Africa, the most prominent ones being the black and green mambas.

The eastern green mamba is a highly venomous snake native to the coastal regions of East Africa. It has a slender build with bright green back scales. The green mamba can grow to six feet in length, and contrary to legend, it is in fact a shy and elusive creature that usually remains hidden in trees, where it preys on birds, rats, and arboreal rodents. Audubon had five green mambas during my tenure. This is not an animal you want to escape from its enclosure.

The reptile building was designed so all the poisonous snakes in the collection were housed in compartments that contained glass on the side of the viewing public and access doors for the keepers in the rear. All the access doors opened into a common room, which was separated from the access to the other exhibits in the building. Only veteran keepers and curators were permitted to enter the poisonous snake room to ensure that security measures were strictly followed and that there would be no possibility of a poisonous reptile gaining access to the other sections of the building. Additionally, the reptile building contained a manually activated snake alarm that sounded a loud wail, signaling that a poisonous snake was outside its enclosure and causing the building to be sealed while any members of the public inside it were herded outside.

This is the way I remember one terrifying morning. I was in the offices of the animal staff, which were located at the far end of the administration building, when I heard an alarm go off. Having never heard the snake alarm go off, I did not know exactly what it was signaling. The general curator was not in his office that day, but the curator of reptiles, Kevin Bowler, was, and he immediately knew that the sound could mean only that one of the poisonous snakes was outside its exhibit. Kevin was an extremely knowledgeable and experienced curator who, on his summer vacations, often collected rattlesnakes, so when he jumped up from his desk, I knew something was wrong.

As he ran to leave the administration building, Kevin called for me to join him, saying he might need every available staff member to handle whatever awaited him in the reptile building. Before I could reiterate to him what he already knew—namely, that I was not a member of the animal staff—I found myself running after him on the way to the reptile house. As he ran, Kevin was on the radio with his staff trying to understand why the alarm had been activated and what was the current situation regarding security in the building. Fortunately, the zoo had not yet opened, so no guests were inside.

When we got to the reptile house, one of the keepers told us that he believed one of the green mambas had somehow escaped its enclosure as he could count only four snakes instead of five looking through the glass from the public viewing area. When he realized this, he immediately activated the snake alarm and sealed off the reptile room while he searched the public areas for the snake. The keeper seemed confident that the snake was not in any public area and had been contained in the poisonous snake holding room. Kevin turned off the alarm and instructed the keeper to stop anyone else from entering the building. Then he and I went to the access door of the poisonous snake room.

Kevin said we would have to enter the containment room and search for the mamba. I thought, What do you mean "we," Kemosabe? Clearly, I was in the wrong place at the wrong time! I emphasized to Kevin that I didn't know the first thing about capturing snakes and surely there must be someone, anyone, more qualified than me to assist in this dubious venture. Kevin said he would be the one searching for and catching the snake and he needed me in the room only in case he was bitten, at which time I would become responsible for getting him out of the room, resealing it, and calling an ambulance to get him to the hospital. What!? Get him out of the room? Reseal the room? You've got to be kidding! Kevin told me not to worry and went to get the protective equipment and tools he would need to enter the restricted room. He retrieved long boots, a face shield, gloves, and a long pole with a hook on the end. I had nothing but my zoo uniform and sneakers!

Slowly, Kevin opened the door. He then looked up to be certain the snake had not crawled on top of or to the side of the door. It looked clear, and he entered the room, beckoned me to enter behind him, and closed the door with both of us inside. I was petrified. Around the room were glass aquariums that held food for the snakes, large plastic drums that served who knows what purpose, a center table, and, most important, a series of doors that led to the exhibits for the other poisonous snakes.

Slowly and methodically, Kevin began to search the room. He looked in every corner, behind every movable glass case, on the floor, in those drums, and in other food containers as he made his way around the room. Me? I stood with my back to the access door, watching and praying Kevin would not find anything and that nothing would come my way.

The search must have lasted only fifteen minutes; I thought it went on for hours. Finally, Kevin made his way completely around the room and back to where I was standing. "I can't find anything," he exclaimed. "If the mamba is in this room, I can't find it. Let's go outside into the corridor, and I'll investigate the exhibit." We exited the room (not soon enough for me), sealed the door, and went into the corridor. When we got to the exhibit, Kevin pointed out the mambas, which were intertwined on a small tree part that the keepers had put in the exhibit to mimic the snakes' natural environment. It was hard to see their heads because they were so enmeshed with one another. After a few minutes, Kevin turned to me and said, "They're all there. It's extremely difficult to see because the five of them are so packed together, but they're all in there."

We were both relieved. I was shaking from the experience, but Kevin looked unperturbed. I guess that comes from handling snakes your whole life. I seldom entered the reptile house again.

The Lost Dog

Dating back to the industrial age, parks have been places of respite and relaxation, places where you can play sports or enjoy the flowers. They are also weird places where all kinds of strange things happen. During my time at Audubon Park, I helped emergency responders pull a man out of one of our lagoons who had drowned after a late-night swim, and I threw people who were protesting the renovation of the golf course over barricades. My security staff broke up disagreements between bicyclers and joggers, skateboarders and people pushing baby carriages. We helped people get married in the park and caught vandals who damaged shelters and tore up flower beds. And we had lots of animal interactions, from unleashed dogs to people who tried to feed the alligators and raccoons. The following story stands out because it is, in fact, very weird.

On an overcast day, a distraught woman came to see me concerning the disappearance of her German shepherd dog. She told me she was walking her dog in the park when it began raining heavily. The dog was not on a leash as the law requires, and she could not corral the animal to take him home in the pouring rain. Apparently, the dog entered an open drainage culvert and was washed into the pipe. The lady was highly upset, telling me that the German shepherd was a beloved family pet and she and her children were beside themselves with grief. She was a professional woman and made it a point to tell me her husband was a lawyer, so I understood the gravity of the situation. She also told me that her dog was purebred and very expensive to acquire. She stated that because the culvert had no cover, which allowed her dog to be washed into the pipe, we were responsible and had to buy her family a new dog—not that that would truly compensate for the loss of the family companion.

I visited the site and confirmed that the culvert indeed had no cover, park staff probably having removed it to clean the pipe and then failed to reattach it. How a fully grown German shepherd could have been washed down the pipe in a rainstorm was not clear, but the evidence of the open culvert was there, and we were responsible for the loss of the dog. I apologized, settled for several thousand dollars to allow the family to purchase a new German shepherd puppy, and even paid for some basic dog training lessons, which the lady said her previous dog had received. I thought that was the end of it. No such luck!

About a month later, the same woman came to my office and somewhat sheepishly showed me a picture of what appeared to be a German shepherd dog, very badly beaten down and malnourished. She told me it was the same dog that had been sucked down the drain—apparently, it had been thrown against the metal screens that guard the intake pumps at a drainage pumping station and somehow survived. After a long month, the dog had made its way back to his house. At first, the family did not recognize the animal, something I could understand having seen the photograph, but finally realized it was their dog and immediately took him to their veterinarian. The poor animal required extensive treatment and rehabilitation before he was reunited with the family. It was, of course, very expensive, and the woman once again demanded that I pay, this time for the veterinary care as well as for psychological counseling for herself and her family to help them recover from this horrible experience. Since the dog was not chipped, it was impossible to tell if the injured animal was in fact her original dog, which I had already paid to replace. Now I was being asked to pay for extensive veterinary care for the dog and psychological counseling for the family. Of course, the threat of a lawsuit loomed in the background.

Often, parks pay for damages to bicycles if they crash on a park pathway or for a trip to the emergency room if a child is hurt because a piece of play equipment fails, but never in my experience had a park paid for a new pet and then paid for the original pet that the new pet was supposed to replace! Let alone counseling.

We paid for the veterinary care but not the psychological counseling. That was sufficient as the family decided not to pursue legal action but instead chose to enjoy both dogs!

So You Want to Build an Aquarium

The Audubon Nature Institute opened the Aquarium of the Americas on the Mississippi River at the edge of the French Quarter in 1990. Aquariums were becoming the family tourist attraction du jour for cities hoping to redevelop their downtowns or waterfront areas. Baltimore had led this initiative by opening its aquarium (now known as the National Aquarium) in 1981 in an urban renewal area focused on its Inner Harbor.

After an extensive planning, permitting, and fundraising effort, the New Orleans aquarium opened to rave reviews, which further impressed upon other cities the potential of an aquarium to bring tourists to town and be the catalyst for the redevelopment of rundown or abandoned areas. One of the cities extremely interested in such a development was Fort Lauderdale, Florida.

Not long after the Aquarium of the Americas (the New Orleans aquarium's official name) opened, Ron Forman, Audubon's CEO, came into my office at the zoo and said that a group of boosters in Fort Lauderdale had contacted him inquiring about how Audubon got started on its aquarium journey and how its fundraising goals had been realized. They were planning to have a fundraising event to raise money to begin planning their aquarium and wanted Ron to come to Fort Lauderdale and make a presentation to their group. Unfortunately, he had a conflicting commitment and could not attend on the date they had scheduled, but he suggested I could go and represent him. Ron asked me whether I felt comfortable talking about the development of our aquarium to a small group of boosters and could I go to Fort Lauderdale. Although I did not have detailed knowledge about all the fundraising efforts, the permitting process and some of the public fundraising efforts were familiar territory. He told the boosters I was coming.

On a Friday, I flew into Fort Lauderdale, went to my hotel, and changed into a suit before leaving for the address Ron had given me where the fundraising event was to be held. To my surprise, the address was not an office building or a museum, hotel, or other event venue. It was a private residence—but not just any private residence. The briefing was at the home of Guy Harvey. I didn't know Guy Harvey from Guy Fieri, but I learned that this Guy Harvey was a world-famous environmentalist and an active ambassador for marine conservation who had established a research institute and ocean foundation. He was interested in establishing a world-renowned aquarium in Fort Lauderdale and had volunteered his home for the fundraiser.

The event was to start at seven o'clock, so I took a cab to the home, arriving about half an hour before the kickoff. The house was in a beautiful neighborhood and backed on one of Fort Lauderdale's many inland canals. It was a gorgeous home in an upscale location, perfect for a gathering with the objective of getting everyone excited about building an aquarium and raising the funds necessary to support the effort.

Another thing I did not know was that Mr. Harvey was also a world-famous marine wildlife artist. That repository of all knowledge, Wikipedia, states, "His depictions of sea life, especially of sport fish such as marlin, are popular with spearfishermen and have been reproduced in prints, posters, T-shirts, jewelry, clothing, and other consumer items." When I entered the house, that connection became obvious as I saw beautiful paintings, sketches, posters, and other artwork sprinkled throughout. It was like an art gallery for fish!

Mr. Harvey greeted me enthusiastically along with some early arrivals for the event. The caterers were busy all over the first floor and in the backyard by the canal. Soon many people began arriving, and it was clear that I had completely misjudged the nature of the briefing, which I thought might involve a dozen or so prominent people. Before long there were seventy to one hundred people in attendance, flowing through the house and out the back door. It was also clear that I was overdressed. No one had a suit on, at least not a traditional business suit like the one I was wearing. Every male was dressed in a leisure suit in all manner of colors—teal, orange, lime—and the women, also in bold, dramatic colors, all had on pantsuits. And no one had socks on! I felt totally overdressed.

As I spoke with a variety of guests, it also became apparent that this was a gathering of not just a few wealthy donors but the crème de la crème of Fort Lauderdale society. Everyone who was anyone was in attendance, and the event was more of a gala than a briefing. The mayor was there as well as several city council members and many of the city's leading citizens and movers and shakers.

After about an hour of socializing, the host called for the guests to come in from outside and gather in his very large den. I stood on the steps leading to the upstairs so I would be above the crowd for my presentation. Now, I've given presentations to many important people and groups, but I really felt somewhat intimidated. I told the gathering about the history behind the Aquarium of the Americas, how important it was for the city's elected and private leadership to be behind the project, and why it was necessary for this group to generate excitement for the venture. Our aquarium had helped generate other development along our riverfront, which I described, and had increased tourism.

I thought the presentation went well and was enthusiastically received. Then Guy Harvey addressed the crowd. He said was necessary for this group to take the lead in raising the first funds for the project, which would allow planning and financial feasibility studies to proceed. Everybody nodded in agreement, but no one immediately produced a check. Then Harvey kicked it up a notch. He took a sculpture of a fish or a turtle (I couldn't see clearly from my vantage point) and put it on the table. He said the sculpture was worth $25,000 and he was donating it as an auction item. Immediately people started bidding, and in short order, more money was bid than the stated value of the sculpture. Soon pledges and donations were pouring in, and I must believe that more than $100,000 was raised at the party.

After the presentation and Mr. Harvey's donation, the party got into high gear, with plenty of eating and drinking both inside and outside the house. I made my way into the rear yard and was admiring the beautiful houses lining both sides of the canal when I noticed an enormous boat coming up the waterway. The boat barely had two or three feet of clearance on either side, and I was amazed it didn't brush against the sides of the canal. The boat stopped directly in front of Mr. Harvey's property, and guests were invited aboard, where the crew was serving more beverages and food. The boat was a sight to behold even amid the magnificent homes in the neighborhood. Mr. Harvey apparently told some guests that the boat would be sailing out into the ocean and invited anyone who was interested to come along. The boat crew contained several attractive women, and one of the guests told me two of them were nicknamed Bambi and Thumper. I don't know if that was true, but that's what I was told! I was clearly over my head in this crowd, and I made my way back to the house, where Mr. Harvey was signing T-shirts he had designed as party favors. I kept my shirt for years.

On the trip back to New Orleans, I reflected on what I had witnessed. There was nothing but money everywhere you looked: houses, cars, art, boats, and beautiful people in full Florida regalia. I thought, This is truly how the other half lives. Fort Lauderdale now has several aquariums. I don't think they ever built one on the scale of ours, but I can say they were never surpassed in their ability to put on a fundraiser.

Raccoons in the Attic

One of the great advantages of working in a zoo is that you get to know members of the animal staff. In modern zoos, the animal staff tend to be broken down into areas of specialization, such as reptiles, birds, mammals, or even individual habitats. At Audubon, staff who work in the Louisiana Swamp Exhibit take care of a variety of animals that live in Louisiana's wetland and swamp areas. Keepers shoulder the main tasks of feeding, health care, and enrichment activities for the animals under their care, and they are supervised by curators, who have overall responsibility. The top animal staffer who is responsible for all the curators and all the animals and their exhibits is usually called the general curator or, in some situations, the vice president of animal affairs. This person is expected to have extensive knowledge about the entire collection. He or she is the go-to person if you have an animal question.

It so came to pass that after I had been with the zoo for several years, I had occasion to call on that knowledge for a problem at my house. One night, my wife woke me to say that she heard chewing and gnawing behind the walls of our bedroom, which was on the second floor of our house. I'm sure that just about everyone has had mice in their house at one point or another, and some might even have had rats. The mice usually become active at night as they forage for food or chew on wood or some other material behind the wall. We all know that irritating sound. Usually, you put out some sort of poisonous bait or sticky traps and the problem goes away. No big deal.

That's the approach I took. I put out a variety of bait and traps, expecting to take care of the situation in short order. But that didn't happen. The chewing and general movement of animals in our walls and attic didn't stop, and in fact, they seemed to get worse. Finally, my wife said, "You work in a place that has all sorts of animal experts. Why not ask them for help?" Which I did.

Curt Burnette was the zoo's general curator. A lanky Midwesterner, he had a calm demeanor, which was essential for someone in his position, since there was always some sort of situation that, if not an emergency, required immediate attention. His knowledge of animal diets, routines, habits, and peculiarities was unmatched, and he always seemed to know how to solve whatever animal-related problems came his way. He got along great with the veterinary staff and the rest of the nonanimal team and was very approachable. In fact, one Thanksgiving, Pat and I invited Curt and his friend Sarah, also a member of the zoo's staff, to have holiday dinner with our family at the Freeport McMoran Audubon Species Survival Center. I'd gotten to know him well, so I went to see him and explained my situation and the approach that was used to address the problem. He asked a series of questions, and from my answers, he seemed to think my problem was more serious than a couple of rogue mice. He thought I might have raccoons in my attic.

This was a situation I had never contemplated, so I asked Curt what action I should take. He told me he would get a large animal trap and bring it to my house, put bait in the cage, and trap the raccoon when it came to eat. This sounded like a plan, so one Saturday, Curt came to our house with the trap.

At the time, my modest two-story house was connected to a garage by a long corridor building about six feet wide, twenty feet long, and seven feet high, which held a laundry room and bathroom. This corridor connected to the den in the main house. (I say "at the time" because when Hurricane Katrina flooded my neighborhood, the corridor building, den, and garage were heavily damaged and were torn off the main house.) Curt climbed on top of the corridor building, which had a flat roof, and placed the trap on the roof with the bait inside. He was confident that after a few days the raccoon would make its way to the roof, take the bait, and become trapped inside; Curt would then release it in a wildlife area outside the city. The plan seemed logical and workable—except it wasn't.

After a few days, we caught a cat but no raccoon. The racket in our bedroom and throughout the attic went on unabated. Curt moved the trap a few feet and tried new bait but to no avail. Finally, he determined to go into the attic and see if he could catch the varmint.

Sporting a pair of very thick gloves, which the keepers use to handle raccoons in our swamp exhibit (raccoons having very significant teeth!), Curt entered through a small door and made his way around the furnace to the very back of the attic. I was outside the door with a flashlight, and I could see that the raccoon had already done significant damage by eating the insulation and air-conditioning ducts and chewing on exposed wiring. This was far more serious than gnawing on some wood. I heard some movement and an ominous hissing sound.

In a few minutes, Curt emerged from the attic but without the raccoon. He said, "Bob, you have a bad problem. First, there are not one but two raccoons. Second, they are large, fully grown adult animals with large claws and fully engaged teeth. Finally, they are huddled together behind the furnace and are very difficult to get to. When I went to grab one, the second lunged at me, and I only just avoided being bitten."

We closed the attic door and went outside. Curt said it was likely the raccoons had gotten into the attic by getting under the house and climbing up through the structure until they decided to make their home in the attic. He said he could not be sure, because it was dark and they were hard to see, but he thought one of the raccoons could be pregnant, which would be another reason for their aggressive behavior. Pregnant! Curt said he doubted even a pest company would want to take on this problem unless it did not have to capture the raccoons alive.

"What do I do now?" I asked.

Curt said, "Bob, I'm going to tell you the secret of how to deal

with nocuous and invasive large animals that get into your house and cannot be trapped because they are too big, too intelligent, or both." There's a secret? Who knew? He explained, "Your goal should be to make your house too uncomfortable for the animals to stay. Make them want to leave and go to your neighbor's house."

Two thoughts went through my mind. One was that I liked my neighbors, and transferring my problem to them did not seem neighborly. But on further thought, desperate people do desperate things, and I was desperate. The second thought was: How do I make my house so uncomfortable that the raccoons will choose to leave?

Curt said, "Make a lot of noise and racket in the attic, jack up the heater so it gets hot, and be sure to put some treats leading to the area you think they used to get into the attic. That should convince them to leave. Then board up the entry openings to keep them from coming back."

This was the secret? Having no better options, I decided to take Curt's advice. I knew I had to plan my attack carefully. These raccoons were smart and crafty creatures who had found an ideal home in my attic, and they were not about to give it up without a fight.

I prepared by visiting a local marine supply store and buying two marine foghorns, which gave off an earsplitting sound. Then I rounded up metal pots and pans, which, when banged together, sounded like a John Philip Sousa marching band gone nuts. Searching through my music collection, I came across a Cher album that included songs like "If I Could Turn Back Time," "Believe," and "Take Me Home," among others. (Remember, it was the 1990s.) If I turned the stereo up full blast, those songs made quite a racket. Finally, I knew I needed help, so I enlisted my thirteen-year-old son Ryan as a partner in the attack.

Saturday morning came, and as Curt advised, we planned to attack early in the day when the raccoons were just settling in. When my wife left the house, we implemented our battle plan. First, I turned up the stereo system as loud as it would go and put Cher to work. The noise was like being in the front row of one of Cher's concerts. Then we sprinkled treats at the location I thought the animals had used to enter the house. We took off the registers on the air-conditioning vents, stuck the air horns inside two of them, and turned them on. It sounded like a boat was about to crash into our house and the coast guard was warning everyone away—an unbelievable sound. Finally, Ryan and I took the pots and pans, went up to the second floor, and ran around banging them together and yelling at the top of our lungs. What a scene! Total chaos! During the engagement, one of our neighbors came over to see what was going on since he had heard all the noise and thought maybe there was a domestic dispute or a murder happening.

We carried on for a good ten minutes of ear-shattering noise. The culmination of our plan involved turning the furnace on as high as it would go (despite the fact it was in the seventies outside) and turning the blowers on full speed. Soon it was like a sauna upstairs. Ryan and I left the house and waited outside, not knowing if our assault would be effective.

But it didn't take long before we saw two gigantic raccoons walk slowly out from under our house and into the open lane in the backyard. They walked nonchalantly away and down the block. Thank goodness they didn't immediately walk under our neighbor's house and try to gain entry. I grabbed some boards and boarded up the entryway to the area underneath our house.

Ryan and I congratulated each other on ridding our house of the unwanted guests. Over the years, I have passed Curt's secret method along to friends who had a variety of uninvited animals, and it has always been a resounding success. My guess, though, is that Cher was often replaced by the Rolling Stones, Metallica, AC/DC or some other noisemaker of choice.

Epilogue

Pat and I have lived most of our adult lives in the South. As you know from reading this book, we grew up in the North, Pat in Johnson City, New York, and myself in Buffalo, New York. Our children were born in New Orleans and consider themselves Southerners.

Growing up in New York State, I often used the phrase "going south" to describe a situation that was deteriorating or in decline. For instance, when I played baseball and we were being beaten badly, I might have said, "This game is going south!" Or when I was taking a calculus exam, I might have thought to myself, My grade is going south. Sometimes I even said, "Buffalo is going south" when reports of factory closings or lost jobs were publicized. You get it. It is a derogatory phase. It means bad things are happening.

Then we moved south, but I never tied the phrase to my new life actually living in a Southern town. I did not think that because we had moved south my life was in decline or that Southerners were still reliving the Civil War and I wouldn't be able to relate to them. (Of course, some still are.) I discovered that Southerners often used the same term to describe some event in their life that was "going south."

In the more than fifty years I have lived in the South, I have never heard someone born in the South say something was "going north." You might go on a trip north, but no one ever says that an event or happening is "going north." No one ever comments that an event in their life went west or east, for that matter. Only "going south" seems to have negative connotations.

Now that the city of Buffalo is experiencing something of a turnaround from its reputation as a Rust Belt city to one that has affordable housing, a revitalized downtown, and a thriving cultural scene, maybe the phrase "going north" is going to catch on! If so, be sure to "Billeve" in Buffalo just as the fanatical Buffalo Bills fan base does.

We have enjoyed living in New Orleans, and hopefully you got that impression from the stories in this book. The city has embraced my family, and I, in turn, have tried to make the city a better place while having some of the most unique experiences imaginable. "Going south" has led to a rich and fulfilling life.

The next time you find yourself saying that one thing or another has "gone south," remember, it's just a saying, and one day it could all "go north"!